STEP UP YOUR

GAME

STEP UP YOUR GAME

A PLAYBOOK FOR THE NEXT GENERATION HERO

SHARM SCHEUERMAN

Advantage®

Published by Advantage, Charleston, South Carolina.
Member of Advantage Media Group.

ADVANTAGE is a registered trademark and the Advantage colophon is a trademark of Advantage Media Group, Inc.

Printed in the United States of America.

ISBN: 978-1-59932-244-5
LCCN: 2010917770

To my wife, Kathy,

and

To my children, Greg, Tom and Jamey,
and my grandchildren, Grace and Will.

ACKNOWLEDGEMENTS

Rarely does one get to thank all of the people who have played such a significant role in your life.

First among them, I would like to thank Jenna Huisken, my ghostwriter and scribe, and part of BCI's creative team, Ballas Creative. You have helped BCI since our inception with your incredible ability to articulate, in my voice, the BCI mission and vision.

Also, I'd like to thank my friend Pat Williams, also an author, who made the introduction to our publishing company, Advantage Media Group in Charleston, SC.

For the players who played for me at the University of Iowa, with Athletes in Action and BCI, and for the players I've helped recruit over the years, I thank you for the influence you have had in my life.

I'd like to thank the Ballas Creative team, Scully and Kit Balasopoulov. You, along with Jenna, have built and protected the Basketball Club International brand from the beginning.

I especially want to thank Carl Cain, my former Iowa Hawkeye teammate. You have had tremendous influence in my spiritual growth.

Thanks to TJ Doyle, my "right hand man" who has always volunteered to step up and help BCI. Your energy, wisdom, faith, and relationship skills have helped promote our organization in incredible ways.

To Eric Lautenbach and NIKE, thank you for your sponsorship of BCI over the last six years.

I wish to thank FCA (Fellowship of Christian Athletes), our valued affiliate. Thanks also to AIA (Athletes in Action) for helping to reveal the Lord's path for me and giving me the experience I needed to make BCI happen.

I offer thanks to the dear friends I've known through NCAA, AIA, Young Life, BCI, bible study, church, sports announcing, and everyday life. You've touched me, and you know who you are.

Finally, and most of all, I am thankful for Kathy. You are so precious to me, beyond words.

CONTENTS

FOREWORD BY GLEN WHISBY 11

INTRODUCTION 13

CHAPTER ONE: WHAT'S IN IT FOR ME? 17

CHAPTER TWO: PLAYING IS A PRIVILEGE 21

CHAPTER THREE: I KNOW YOUR NAME 25

CHAPTER FOUR: THEY CAN MAKE NOISE 29

CHAPTER FIVE: YOU ARE SOMEBODY'S HERO 33

CHAPTER SIX: TALKING THE TALK 37

CHAPTER SEVEN: TO THE BEST OF YOUR ABILITY 41

CHAPTER EIGHT: AUTHORITY FIGURES 45

CHAPTER NINE: THE BE ATTITUDE 49

CHAPTER TEN: IS THAT ALL? 53

CHAPTER ELEVEN: VIEW FROM THE BRIDGE 57

CHAPTER TWELVE: JUDGMENT CALL 63

CHAPTER THIRTEEN: TAKING IT PERSONALLY 69

CHAPTER FOURTEEN: TEAM OF BROTHERS 91

CHAPTER FIFTEEN: ICE IN THE VEINS 95

CHAPTER SIXTEEN: INVINCIBLE 99

CHAPTER SEVENTEEN: WHO ARE YOU? 103

CHAPTER EIGHTEEN: RUNNING AWAY 107

CHAPTER NINETEEN: WHICH WAY IS UP? 111

CHAPTER TWENTY: WOMEN & MEN 115

CHAPTER TWENTY-ONE: INJUSTICE 119

CHAPTER TWENTY-TWO: ONE CINDERBLOCK SHORT 125

CHAPTER TWENTY-THREE: TOUGH STREET 129

CHAPTER TWENTY-FOUR: MAKING THINGS RIGHT 133

CHAPTER TWENTY-FIVE: LETTING GO 137

CHAPTER TWENTY-SIX: GAME CHANGERS 141

CHAPTER TWENTY-SEVEN: IMPACT 147

CHAPTER TWENTY-EIGHT: SOON, BUT NOT YET 151

CHAPTER TWENTY-NINE: LOOKING UP 155

CHAPTER THIRTY: REFLECTIONS 159

FOREWORD

I grew up in a small town in Brookhaven, Mississippi, but found opportunities to do some great things. I was selected to be the Gatorade Player of the Year in my home state, I played with Chris Webber and Jason Kidd in the Nike ABCD Camp, and I was MVP in the McDonald's All-American game. The biggest moment in my young life, or so I thought, happened when I went to the Portsmouth Invitational. It was a step just before the NBA. I thought I was ready to go to the next level, but then I had the worst game of my life.

I looked around the stands. I'd just stunk up the place, but now there was a guy who wanted to talk to me. Why would anyone want to talk to me after that game? It was Coach Sharm Scheuerman.

We sat down in the lobby and talked. He opened up a Bible and we looked at it together. I realize now that I'd have given up every other opportunity for that day – the day I connected with Coach Sharm for the first time. It was the beginning of something important, above and beyond the success I'd always pictured for myself.

I went overseas and played professional basketball for 14 years in Italy, Spain, France, and Russia. I've seen the world, playing the game I love, and I'm very grateful for that. During that time, Coach Sharm never lost contact with me. He always told me he'd love to have me play on his team someday. When BCI Edge had an opportunity to play a Christmas tournament in Amsterdam, Coach Sharm asked me to come.

Coach Sharm was a true mentor to me. He took me under his wing, beginning with that day at the Portsmouth Invitational, when I didn't know where I was going. When I went to Chicago with BCI

Edge, Coach gave me the opportunity to pass it on and become a mentor. I had the opportunity to put my arm around a kid and ask, “What do you want to do with your life? Do you know Jesus loves you?” Coach Sharm told me that I was one of his favorites, and I don’t take that lightly. It’s a responsibility to keep his spirit alive and make a difference.

A week before Coach Sharm died, I talked with him as tears rolled down my cheeks. How many of us could sit there and love on people when we are about to die? How many of us would keep comforting and mentoring others at that moment? Coach Sharm said, “Glen, I’m going to be with Jesus. When you know where you’re going, you don’t have to worry.” He wasn’t scared, looking death in the eye. He just didn’t want me to be afraid.

Coach Sharm didn’t worry about himself, or even about basketball. He was concerned about players' lives – the big picture. Your life and career can mean more than you ever imagined, and I’m grateful that he showed me how to pass that message on to you. As Coach always said, “Keep looking up.”

—*Glen Whisby*

INTRODUCTION

The idea for Basketball Club International hit me in 1997, when I was working with Athletes in Action. I saw a need in basketball, at the professional level, for players to really stand out – and stand up – for integrity, character and faith. A place where they could play a top-level game *and* be real heroes to the kids who respect them. I didn't know I was going to be the one to help fill this need, but I knew someone should. I could see it would be tough. If you believe in the Lord, as I do, you'll understand when I say that He's the one who led me to stand up, step up, and make a plan.

One NBA general manager said I'd be "swimming upstream" when I told him my vision. In the basketball business, the general managers, coaches and players exist in separate circles. There's a lot of isolation; business and personal matters don't overlap unless someone – usually a player – gets into trouble off the court. Even then, the league has a reactionary approach, e.g., "Fix it or forget it." Many NBA insiders have lamented the lack of organizational support for the personal, internal lives of the players. Players know *of* each other, but they don't *know* each other. Basketball Club International, a.k.a. BCI, is the solution we offer.

BCI is a professional players' touchstone, a fellowship loop, an international goodwill organization, and a place where young players can become great, real role models. We've been welcomed by so many in professional basketball. Our organization promotes the idea that we can all step up to a legacy we're proud of. We call this idea *Generation Hero.*

Each of us can have an effect on this world every day. I've wanted my life to be a positive influence. And you, whoever you are, can inspire others with your integrity and faith, and with the potential of your youth or the wisdom of your years. Together, we are all connected by character and motivated by love. We can do better – always. We are all Generation Hero.

Being a part of Generation Hero is like being in "the zone." As the game of life carries you, or even throws you for a loop, you stay focused and strong by knowing that you are living a life of worth, based on meaningful values and expressed with a positive attitude. Your enthusiasm for your family, for your faith, and even simply for great basketball makes a difference for everyone you meet. And with a clear head and a powerful heart, you choose this. (And it is your choice, no matter what your circumstances may be.) You say, "The world needs someone like me. I'm ready, and it's my turn to play."

Generation Hero is supported by BCI's U.S. and international athletic events, camps, clinics, partner organization work, and goodwill activities. Wherever you live, whatever your age, and however your life has unfolded so far, you can choose to be a part of this exciting personal and global legacy. The world needs Generation Hero as much as we need it. Whether you are a professional player or a teen, a leader, a parent or guardian, a benefactor, a soldier, or just someone who works and lives, you can do this. To begin, simply start where you are. *Game on.*

I hope that, over the next 10 or 20 years, BCI and Generation Hero become an indispensible part of the professional basketball machine. We want a strong loop of heroes who support one another in a personal, meaningful way. We want these heroes to inspire the younger generation to carry themselves at a level higher, perhaps, than the circumstances that produced them. Allan Houston (NBA All-Pro) asked a group of BCI players at a leadership summit, “Can you imagine what an impact a team like BCI Edge could have worldwide?” I have, and it’s why I put this ball in motion. Now it’s up to BCI, you, and others like you, to take Generation Hero to the next level. The possibilities seem truly incredible.

—*Sharm*

"BCI Edge takes what's great about basketball – the excitement, the fans, the competition – and frames it with a public commitment to ideals. This organization is out there playing a professional-level game… I applaud what they are doing."

—Bob Costas

"When a BCI Edge player lives his life according to principle, leading by example with good character, personal integrity, sportsmanship, and a public commitment to core values, he's earned his right to be an excellent role model."

—William Hybl
Chairman and CEO, El Pomar Foundation

"When BCI competes and mentors, the world benefits from a ripple effect of enthusiasm and faith. They choose to walk the walk, here and now. I stand tall in support of BCI – these guys help all of us raise the bar on what we should expect from professional athletes."

—Allan Houston
NBA All-Star

CHAPTER ONE

WHAT'S IN IT FOR ME?

I saw a pro basketball player on TV the other day. He'd been an All-American and an amazing player. I think he earned $50 million to $60 million over the course of his career. Sounds great, right? How would you like to have that legacy? Is this your picture of a successful man and athlete?

But the news wasn't reporting on his latest great accomplishment. This player was making news because he was bankrupt and, literally, out on the street. I'll bet you don't want *that* legacy. You're probably wondering how anyone could let that happen.

How can someone be so financially successful and then fall so far? Sad to say: easily. This player, like a lot of successful athletes and other people – in sports or not – asked, "What's in it for me?" and expected the world to write him a check.

Now, we've all heard that money doesn't buy happiness. It also doesn't buy respect. Conversely, a lack of it doesn't mean despair. Money is simply something you trade for material things. Nothing more, nothing less. But if something exists outside of your mind and heart, it's not really under your control. If you want all that the world has to offer, you're at the mercy of the world to let you keep it.

I am 76 years old. I have cancer. I know I am going to spend eternity with Jesus. What I have learned, since I was a young man asking, "So, what's in it for me, anyway?" is that the question only gets a good response if you pose it to the right source. Here's what I mean:

QUESTION #1:

You: "World, I'm awesome. If I serve your desires, what's in it for me?"
The world: "Riches, or nothing, or both. And I can change my mind at any time, so don't get comfortable."

QUESTION #2:

You: "Jesus, if I have a personal relationship with you, what's in it for me?
Jesus: "Peace of mind. A promise of eternal life. And these are yours forever, no matter what happens."

Have you heard the story of King Solomon? He was probably the richest man ever. "Vanity, vanity, all is vanity," he said at the end of his life, rich with possessions, but poor inside himself. "What's it worth?" What's it worth, indeed. We are all just wisps of smoke that are here for a little while and then gone from this life forever. So who will we be while we're here? What are we worth, here?

As for me, I've been successful, I've hit walls, I've bounced back, and now I'm dealing with disease – and that's just the way life goes. But in my heart, I've learned what's important – no matter what happens. When you are where I am, looking back on your whole life, you will have wisdom to pass on. Think about what that wisdom will be. What is the question you would have asked, if you had known to ask it? What is the question you'll want your grandchildren to ask?

Through my journey in life, I've been changed by God. It didn't feel like a lightning bolt; it felt like a bunch of them. The question to ask, when you're young and have your life spread before you, isn't, "How much can I get?" but, "How much can I give?" You still have time. It's never too late to start working through the big questions. But don't put it off, because it's never too early, either. What's it all worth? What do you want it to be worth? What are *you* really worth?

Of course, I'm not talking about money. You can't trade that for real security, or real love, or real happiness. Money doesn't make you a man. In fact, if that's all you're after, you could end up shortchanging the legacy you could have had in this world.

All people have their own story about what made them, and about what made them whole. As I take the opportunity to share my story, I'll be asking you about your story-in-development. Wherever you are on your journey, I hope these chapters get you excited about what's ahead for you.

> *Don't become so well-adjusted to your culture that you fit into it without even thinking. Instead, fix your attention on God. You'll be changed from the inside out.*
>
> —Romans 12:2 (The Message)

YOUR TURN

List your dreams for the future. Now list your fears for the future.

If your dreams came true, and then your worst fears came true, what would be left of you? What's your real worth?

CHAPTER TWO

PLAYING IS A PRIVILEGE

Some kids grow up with a father in their lives. Some do not. I had a taste of both worlds, because my father passed away suddenly when I was in ninth grade.

Dad was a contractor, and we had a field across from where he had built our house – an overgrown pasture. My brother, Tom, and I, along with a few friends, decided to make a baseball field there. We had push lawnmowers, not the power kind, and so we worked hard cutting the grass down with a sickle before pushing the mower as far as we could push. We'd make it six feet before we'd have to start over again with the sickle. After a lot of hard work, we finally had a baseball field. Dad was so impressed that he poured concrete and installed a basket in one part of our clearing to make a basketball court, too.

Naturally, we spent a lot of time playing there, but the best part was when Dad got home from work. Soon after we heard his truck pull up, we'd yell, "Come play, Dad!" He would be incredibly tired from his job, but we'd be clamoring for his attention. As tired as he was, he came into our field to hit balls with us until dinner.

Not that Dad was all about playing. I had to sweep the driveway before I was allowed to practice basketball. I had to water the lawn before I could play baseball in the summers. Every morning, Tom and I had to fill a basket of pulled water grass before we could play ball. Chores came first.

I learned from Dad that playing sports is a privilege. Just like being a father, or a father figure, is a privilege. In both cases, you earn it over and over again. You show up in the field to play. You show up every day and you're grateful for it. It never becomes a right.

I wish Dad had been around during my high school and college years, because he loved athletics and would have gotten a kick out of the competitive atmosphere I found at the University of Iowa under head basketball coach Bucky O'Connor. Luckily, I had my father's friends and then Bucky to guide me and push me through those years. It wasn't enough to keep me out of trouble entirely, but those men, along with my mom, gave me a great support system. I learned to be accountable to others.

Now, with Basketball Club International's professional team, BCI Edge, I counsel many players who, from a young age, have been handed attention and success based exclusively on their basketball abilities. Growing up like that, it can be easy for some pro-level players to think, "I have a right to be here. I earned this myself and I'm grateful only to myself."

Guys with that attitude can be difficult to coach, because they think that everyone wants a piece of them. After a recent trip to China with our BCI Edge team, I had a conversation with a young player who seemed to have trouble with authority figures – especially coaches.

I asked him, "Why do you think a guy my age is worried about a guy like you? Why would I help you become a better player and a better man? What do I gain by it? Don't you think I have other things to do if you're not going to be receptive?"

What could he say? What would you say?

If you look at athletic talent as a privilege, or if you look at your other qualities as privileges, then the world may begin to look a little different to you. You may start telling the difference between what's for your own good and what's for your own ego. You can stop taking your situation for granted. Work hard (and earn some respect). Listen up (and show *a lot* of respect).

Also – if your father wasn't, or isn't, available to you physically or emotionally, you probably learned to look out for yourself. But you can't be your own father figure, no matter how hard you try or how wise you are. Find good people, and then start building relationships you can count on. When someone feels privileged to know you, and you feel privileged to know him or her – that's a great start.

Playing and coaching basketball was my privilege. Being part of the Fabulous Five back at Iowa was a privilege. With great privilege comes great responsibility – especially in "giving back" or "passing it on." So I'm doing both now, through Basketball Club International and our team, BCI Edge, and I try to use my accomplishments to shine a light on others.

Don't lose your grip on Love and Loyalty. Tie them around your neck; carve their initials on your heart. Earn a reputation for living well in God's eyes and the eyes of the people.

—Proverbs 3:3-4 (The Message)

YOUR TURN

Think about your special strengths and talents. Looking at these as your own set of privileges, how will you use them in your life and in the lives of others?

CHAPTER THREE

I KNOW YOUR NAME

When I was 6 years old, I was playing on the living room floor when my Dad's business partner came in and said, "Hi, Sharm." Without so much as looking up I replied, "Hi," and went back to playing. Immediately, my father took me into the back bedroom and gave me the spanking of my life. He said, "You never just say 'hi' to someone you know. If you know someone's name, you always call them by name."

I never forgot it. Even now, I try to call people by name whenever I can. Not to avoid spankings, of course, but because it will make them feel recognized as a person. I do it to let them know that I respect their presence in my life at that moment. Name tags do help, though.

The significance of personal acknowledgement hit me personally as a sophomore in high school. I was brought up to the varsity basketball team at the end of my sophomore season to play in a season-ending game against the Davenport Blue Devils. Right across the Mississippi River from my hometown of Rock Island, Ill., Davenport had won many, many Iowa state championships. As we were in the same Quad City Conference with Davenport, we played them twice every year – tough, hard-fought games. The margin of victory was never more than three points that year. I knew all of the players' names because they were some of my heroes – especially Kenny Buckles.

Kenny was a Davenport senior who had been All-State in Iowa for three years. We've all known a guy like that, a couple years older who's a better player than you at that time. Kenny was that guy and I was awed by him.

I got into this game near the end because I could press and was quick. As Kenny was going in for a layup, I made a clean block as he was going up. As the official handed him the ball for his inbounds pass, Kenny looked me in the eye and said, "Nice block, kid."

Sure, he didn't use my name, but he acknowledged me. I felt like I was *somebody*. I think we lost the game by three points, but oh boy, Kenny Buckles recognized me. He saw what I did. My world sure seemed to take an upturn that night by his simple act of recognition. Kenny went on to play for the Hawkeyes, as I did. When he was a senior at Iowa, we shared starting assignments. Imagine what a thrill that was to be on the same ball club with my early hero.

Acknowledging someone's name or accomplishment is a simple way to show respect. And it's nice when they return the favor. It's part of creating personal connections in life. It's a way of saying, "I see you. You matter."

When I gave my life to Jesus, years later as an adult, I felt acknowledged by Him in a way that no person could ever do. He took me just as I was. This is a special thing about having a personal relationship with Jesus. When He says, "I see you, I love you, and I know your name," He really means it. He only asks that you see Him and love Him back.

While we were yet sinners, Christ died for us.

—Romans 5:8 (New American Standard)

He knew my name.

YOUR TURN

Do you acknowledge other people's names? What about their accomplishments? Their setbacks? Make it a point to try.

CHAPTER FOUR

THEY CAN MAKE NOISE

Two years before the events in the movie *Hoosiers*, in the spring of 1952, there was a little high school named Hebron that beat all of the bigger schools to win the Illinois basketball state championship. Almost everyone in the state was rooting for this little team to finally have its day. Of course, my Rock Island teammates and I wanted to take them down. It was our job.

In the state final four, we got our chance, and it was like walking into a hornet's nest. It seemed the entire population of Champaign, Ill., and beyond was against us. If this had been a movie, Rock Island would have been the bad guys – the bigger school that didn't have a compelling, underdog story.

Looking at the enthusiastic crowd, I thought, "They can boo and they can make as much noise as they want, but they can't step across the inbound line. They can't get on the court. They have to stay in the stands."

Sure, it's nice when the little guy wins. But my Rock Island team wasn't interested in creating a feel-good story for the Midwestern press.

We knew we weren't actually on the *wrong* side, as some fans seemed to suggest. We were just there to win, just like any team would be. So we played harder, fueled by the fans' attitudes against us. I know I did. We lost, but it wasn't due to a lack of effort.

Hebron went on to win the state title with an overtime victory over Quincy. This was back when schools of different sizes competed for a single championship. The town of Hebron painted its water tower to resemble a basketball, commemorating the 1952 championship. Inside the high school, their state title trophy is displayed along with the court's center circle, removed from the court to commemorate the season.

Even many years later, Hebron's story inspired a book, *Once There Were Giants: How Tiny Hebron Won the Illinois State Championship and the Hearts of Fans Forever* by Johnson and Kistler, and a documentary film. This continued celebration was inevitable.

Also inevitable: when the two top players from Hebron ended up at the University of Illinois, I made it my goal to get back at them whenever Iowa played them. I recalled Rock Island's bitter defeat to Hebron every single time I guarded those guys, especially Paul Judson – a great college player – and it sure inspired fierce competitiveness on my part.

At Iowa, in fact, over our three years our away record was better than our home record. It must have been the booing and the crowd. We just were inspired to play harder.

There are a few places where people feel pretty free to root against you. In sports and politics, of course, but also in the area of one's personal spiritual life. But while opposition in sports and politics is usually public and outspoken, welcoming a strong response, opposition to one's personal beliefs can often be more subtle – and harder to combat.

Even though my mother and father raised me as a Christian, it wasn't until I was in my 40s that I realized something was missing in my life. That big void was a personal relationship with Jesus. I wanted to know more about that. I wanted to be around people who also wanted to know more. So I had to make a decision: stay with the large, well-established, well-connected church that didn't have exactly what I needed, or find a group, however small, that would help me on my personal journey toward God.

It's difficult to leave what you know, but I had to. I may not have had others booing my decision directly, but most people don't get cheered for bucking the mainline system and trying something new.

My wife, Kathy, and I started attending a small church that held meetings in the basement of a Masonic building, where they preached about a personal relationship with Jesus. This was just what we needed. We were able to grow stronger in our faith because of this decision.

In a way, we've joined His team, which means that it doesn't matter who's making noise against us. We know what we have to do, in His name, and we're here to play.

So when you're on the court or anywhere else, and you've got a game to play, a job to do, or choices to make, you're going to hear some noise. Sometimes they're cheering for you, and that's a great feeling. Maybe everyone is rooting against you, which can feel like a real hornet's nest. Either way, remember that it's just noise. Listen to yourself – and your coach – instead.

Every word of God is flawless;
He is a shield to those to take refuge in Him.

—Proverbs 30:5 (New International Version)

YOUR TURN

How do you summon strength in the face of opposition? Are you able to stand up against the noise of the crowd?

How did Jesus react to the noise and opposition to Him?

CHAPTER FIVE

YOU ARE SOMEBODY'S HERO

In sixth grade, I was getting very interested in basketball. From our church, my dad knew Hub Wagner, a great man and the basketball coach at Rock Island High School, so he asked if my brother and I could watch their practices over Christmas break. The school was otherwise empty – barren, in fact – which added to our excitement. Just think: the Rock Island High School basketball team, plus Tom and Sharm.

The coach let us stand under the basket to catch balls and throw them back to the players as they shot. We knew this was a very special role – hanging out with the big guys, our heroes, who played in the big gym. We came back to help a couple more times that Christmas break.

The Rock Island High School basketball players were my heroes. Like Kenny Buckles later, they were older kids who played as good as I hoped I could play someday. Kids who made me want to grow up and play a great game, too.

I thought I would have died and gone to heaven just to play basketball for the Rock Island High School Rocks – to play on that big court where my heroes played. I realize now that the thrills I had playing there a few years later were every bit as huge for me as I had playing in NCAA championships. I wonder if those high school players realized what an impact, what an influence, they had on this wide-eyed sixth grader who idolized them.

Jesus set a great example for all of us, with unconditional love and sacrifice. I look to Him as I develop myself in this world. He's my personal hero.

Recently, at an event in Alabama with Basketball Club International, I noticed that the kids seemed surprised that professional basketball players would spend time with them, without pay or recognition. They were awed that these heroes from BCI Edge happened to actually care about them.

I remind BCI Edge players, and NBA stars I talk to, not to take this hero thing for granted. I also remind the kids I meet at basketball clinics around the world. I want them, and you, to remember that someone is looking up to you right now. It doesn't matter how old you are, or what you think you've accomplished in life. Someone sees something special in you and wants to be like you.

"A hero is someone who understands the responsibility that comes with his privilege"

—Me

YOUR TURN

Who were your first heroes? What did they do right that you admired? What could they have done differently?

Now, look around and identify someone who looks up to you. Be specific. Now think of three things you can do, or say, to show that you take that privilege seriously.

CHAPTER SIX

TALKING THE TALK

Bucky O'Connor, the head basketball coach of the University of Iowa Hawkeyes for seven seasons (1950 and 1952-1958), was a popular guest speaker at high school graduation ceremonies, University of Iowa alumni events, fundraisers, awards ceremonies, service club functions such as Kiwanis and Rotary, and national coaching clinics. He was a great coach and everyone wanted to hear him. He was a natural, on and off the stage. I remember walking down the street with Bucky, who never missed an opportunity to greet people, and asking him, "Why do you talk to everybody we pass?" He said, "It's just as easy to speak to them as it is to avert." I've thought about that little comment a lot. I've always been an introvert, but I've also always wanted to have Bucky's ease with people.

When Coach was tragically killed in an automobile accident in 1958, I inherited the leadership of the team and the challenge to live up to his legacy on court and in front of the crowds. At 24 years old, I was the youngest Big Ten head basketball coach ever. I was energetic and committed to my new role. However, when I also inherited his remaining speaking engagements – at least 30 events across Iowa and Illinois that spring – I knew it would be a big challenge.

I had a stutter, and I avoided using *N* and *L* sounds. Very few people outside close friends and family knew about it. I was better with small, familiar groups.

Bill Schoof, a teammate and always a funny guy, would sometimes ask me in front of girls when we played at other schools, "Sharm, where does your brother go to school?" Well, he went to Northwestern and I couldn't say it without putting a couple of "uhs" in front of it. So I would say, "Tom goes to uh-Northwestern." Of course, to embarrass me, Bill would ask, "Where's uh-Northwestern?"

I'd been married for quite a few years before I finally told my father-in-law, a judge in Clinton, Iowa, about my stutter. He said, "I never knew you had a stutter. I just thought you chose your words delicately."

It was true that I was careful with my words, sometimes using phrases to substitute words I knew would be challenging for me. But often it was necessary to use a tough word, like asking a telephone operator for "La Porte City." You couldn't just dial a number directly like you can today – back then you needed to speak with an operator to make a long distance call. I'd hang up seven or eight times before I could get it right for the switchboard.

I'd gone to a speech clinic in Rock Island, and one at the University of Iowa, where Wendell Johnson – a world-renowned speech therapy expert who became a good friend – taught me to draw an invisible line on my pants to help me begin difficult words.

Despite the help, I dreaded getting up in front of a crowd – especially a crowd that should have been listening to a great speech from Coach O'Connor.

I remember driving to many events, spending much time in prayer: "Lord, I don't want to do this but there's no way I can get out of it." I would prepare bullet points on the back of my invitation in advance, often making extra notes during the event before it was my turn to speak. I drew lines on my pants and tried to give it my best effort. In a way, it was a competitive thing – a personal challenge I knew I had to overcome. I was doing this for Coach, for the University of Iowa, and for myself.

The more talks I gave, the more comfortable and confident I felt. I could tell a couple of funny stories to soften up the crowd. I could refer to local sports heroes and poke fun at some of the locals. I could give advice from the heart and not think so much about which words I'd have to avoid using.

Coach was a beloved figure, and he was like a second father to me. I often spoke of him in my talks and I'd sometimes say, "I'd rather be in the audience with you listening to Coach Bucky than up here talking."

My feeling about that never changed, but I learned that sometimes when you're forced to do something you really don't want to do, you can get kind of good at it. You can make it work. Although, I remember getting a note from a school where I'd spoken twice: once in that first year and again five years later. It read, "Sharm, you've improved!" I thought, "Just how bad was I before?"

After my coaching career, I did color commentary on radio and TV for the Iowa Television Network. It was for a much bigger audience, but it felt more like a conversation. Jim Zabel, an experienced radio commentator who became my radio mentor, made it especially fun.

Nowadays, I don't have much trouble with stuttering, but it's been a lifelong work in progress. Choosing my words carefully is as much a habit as ever, but for less self-conscious reasons.

Overcoming personal challenges often takes pushing through real fear over and over again. The alternative is turning your back on your responsibilities, and you can't do that. There are calls – and tests – you can't ignore.

I can do all things through Him who strengthens me.

—Philippians 4:13 (New International Version)

YOUR TURN

What personal challenges or fears do you have? How can you work on them?

Have you turned your back on something important because you were afraid of not "getting it right" the first time?

Where do you find the strength to overcome your fears?

CHAPTER SEVEN

TO THE BEST OF YOUR ABILITY

Before the game, I remember standing at the free throw line as they introduced both teams – the Iowa Hawkeyes and the San Francisco Dons – shut off the lights, and played the "Star Spangled Banner." We were about to compete in the finals of the 1956 NCAA championship. I thought of the hundreds of thousands, or millions, of kids who would give anything to be in my shoes at that very moment.

In the dark, I said a prayer: "Lord, help me play to the top of my ability so that when the game is over, I can walk off the court and say, 'I gave it my all. I couldn't have played any harder.' " I wasn't too far along on my spiritual path, but I knew enough to pray for this. Not for a win, but for my best effort.

Once, a friend confided in me that he sometimes had an empty feeling, even after winning a championship. That wasn't the case for me. Even though we didn't win, I truly felt I had played up to my capabilities. My internal goal for the game was satisfied, even if my external goal wasn't.

I see a lot of pressure on kids at the AAU level, for junior high and high school basketball players. Kids used to play for their own school.

Now coaches take any top players they can get, from any school, and play all summer in front of college recruiters. The goal is to win, and second place doesn't get you anything. It's great when parents are looking for scholarships, but I've heard a lot of kids say, "I have to win or else my parents or coach will chew me out. My life will be ruined."

Getting caught up in the pressure to win every single time is never going to bring out a kid's best abilities. The wins will be empty and the losses will be unnecessarily devastating. I think we need to reframe the challenge.

You'll never hear me minimize the drive to be the best. I had that competitive spirit, too, and it's important. But if the other guy is better than you, you've got to accept that. Coaches and parents need to acknowledge it, too. All we can ask – and this is my challenge to both pro players and youths – is that you walk off the court saying, "I couldn't have worked any harder. I played to the best of my ability today." If you keep up that attitude and drive, you'll probably help your team win more games. Plus, you'll earn respect and feel good about yourself, regardless of the score.

Whatever you do, work at it with all your heart,
as working for the Lord, not for men.
—Colossians 3:23 (NIV)

YOUR TURN

List your internal performance goals and external performance goals. How do you balance them?

If you know that you will perform to the absolute best of your ability, how will it affect your experience of competition?

CHAPTER EIGHT

AUTHORITY FIGURES

I once coached a basketball player who, while 6'4" and a great athlete, had played at four schools because he couldn't get along with the coaches anywhere. During one of our regular team times, he said, "I've never been able to trust male authority figures. I didn't know my father growing up, and I didn't get respect from any of my coaches. So I never learned how to trust anyone. My lack of trust has certainly proved to be a detriment to my basketball progress."

Though Antwon had earned a reputation for his rebellious attitude, he and I got along just fine. He trusted me because he knew that, while I didn't always tell him what he wanted to hear, I kept his best interests in mind. We established a mutual respect and trust for each other. He showed a willingness to be coached, and became a better player because of it.

A lot of kids grow up uncertain about who to trust, maturing into adults who are still not knowing. It can be a real challenge, especially for an athlete who feels – from a young age – that everyone seems to want a piece of him. But if that athlete ends his playing days with that same lack of trust, I can promise you it will carry over and continue into the remainder of his life.

So how do you know who to trust?

A lot of players continue to search for that answer. What I learned, especially as a young athlete, is that trust is earned by people who show you they want to earn it. People who only show interest in what you can do for them are not in the business of earning your trust – they're just in business.

A trustworthy person won't always tell you what you want to hear, either. After my father passed away, I learned to rely on his closest friends for advice about my biggest decision up to that time – where to go to college.

I remember the camaraderie between my dad and his three best friends as we piled into a car, bound for the University of Illinois to watch football games in the fall. We'd leave early in the morning and, after four hours, we'd stop to eat lunch in an apple orchard near the stadium. They all smoked cigars, so Tom and I had to sit in the middle seats – Tom in the front and me in the back – to let the men blow smoke out of the windows. I liked them because they were friends of my dad. I saw their loyalty to my parents and I knew I could trust them. During our annual trips in that smoky old car, a bond developed between us boys and Dad's friends that became a lasting and trusting friendship.

We'd always have seats together behind the bench at Augustana College in Rock Island. Our church was kind of the home church for Augustana, and I thought seriously about going to college there so that I could play football, basketball and baseball. It was a great little school – a gem. But I knew in my heart that I'd always wonder whether I could have played in the Big Ten. I'd always wonder, "Was I good enough?"

Bradley University, 90 miles away from home, contacted me when I was a junior in high school, offering me a scholarship. Boy was I excited. I thought it might be a great idea, but I wasn't sure.

My mom would have gone along with whatever I wanted for college. She'd ask me questions about my intentions, but didn't try to sway me. We did spend considerable time in prayer during the process.

Then my dad's friends stepped up. They were concerned about a recent scandal at Bradley that involved point manipulations and player gambling. They knew Bradley was a good school, but despite the scholarship offer, they advised me to look for other opportunities. They encouraged me to pursue my Big Ten dream.

I'm glad I went Big Ten after all. I'm glad I had people in my life who knew my heart, wanted only the best for me in their hearts, and guided me without selfish intentions. I knew I could trust them completely. If I had closed myself off to the authority figures in my life and adopted an attitude of "I can only trust myself now," I would have missed out on some great advice. I wouldn't have weighed my options as wisely. I might have just gone along with the flow.

Some coaches, and even parents, try to make decisions for young players without considering every angle. They might want you to go with their flow – whatever's easiest or "best for everyone." I encourage you, wherever you are in life, to actively seek mentors who don't have a personal stake in your success. I also encourage you to ask your peers who they trust. Many players have found me, and BCI Edge, by referral.

Stakeholders in your success may offer good advice, too, but you must always weigh it against your own values and goals. After a while, you'll know whether you can trust an authority figure. Until then, and even after you establish trust and mutual respect, remember to use your own mind as you consider all of your options.

Trust God from the bottom of your heart; don't try to figure out everything on your own. Listen for God's voice in everything you do, everywhere you go; He's the one who will keep you on track.

—PROVERBS 3: 5-6 (THE MESSAGE)

YOUR TURN

Who are your authority figures? Do you have trouble accepting advice and criticism from authority figures in your life?

Who do you trust? Why?

Who trusts you? Why?

CHAPTER NINE

THE BE ATTITUDE

Do you focus on what you do, or on who you are? In His "Sermon on the Mount" (Matthew 5), Jesus tells us that you are blessed when you're content with just who you are. But many people get hung up on how much they *do* instead. Even devout Christians fall into this trap. I want to tell you that if you are who you are supposed to BE, the *doing* will automatically follow. It doesn't work the other way around.

My brother, Tom, was a great example of *being*. He was my only sibling. Tom and I were close growing up, and very competitive. I was an All-State football quarterback and Tom, while quarterback two years later at our high school, was always known as "Sharm's younger brother." It didn't make him jealous, but it made him want to prove he could be a success in his own right. He wanted to be independent.

Instead of following me to Iowa, Tom chose Northwestern University. He came back to Iowa for law school, and spent many successful years as an attorney for 3M, but by then he wasn't just "Sham's younger brother" anymore. In fact, he'd come into his own and found his personal identity – one that would inspire me to follow a bit in his footsteps!

When Tom decided to be an ambassador for the Lord, he was led to help people "from the inside out." He spent many weekends living among convicted felons in Stillwater, Minn., sharing his faith and inspiring the BE attitude in others. He joined the Young Life organization, a national faith-based group for adolescents and young adults, and served on its national board of directors for almost a decade.

Tom felt called to use his strengths to help people achieve their best potential. So, in a way, he was a coach, too. As an ambassador for Jesus, Tom looked to his "being" to help guide his "doing." His example touched me throughout my whole life, and even inspired me to get involved as a leader in Young Life.

I think we were both greatly influenced by our mother, who was always so concerned about other people and always wanted to share her faith with others.

About two years after Tom retired from 3M, he developed stomach cancer. Three months later, he passed away. Here's what he said to me over and over during his illness: "Sharm, if God cures me of the cancer, what a great story it would be. What a great witness I would be for God here in this world. If not, I'll just be up there waiting for you."

I always felt as if I could beat Tom at anything, but in the spring before he passed away, he won a tennis match against me. We always joked that God had allowed him to stay on earth long enough to finally beat his older brother in tennis.

Tom showed an incredible attitude all the way through his life, and also through his pain. I think he was strong because of who he was. I think he accomplished what he did for the same reason.

The world may tell you what to do, but it can't tell you who to be. In fact, what the world wants from you may be the opposite of who you really are according to your values. But if you decide to BE the best you can be – spiritually, physically, and mentally – your actions will be right on target with who you are. You'll achieve real, lasting success.

And if you decide to be an ambassador for Jesus, you'll know what to do because it's what He would do. Just start by being who He'd be in any situation. It may sound simple, but it works.

We are therefore Christ's ambassadors, as though
God were making His appeal through us.

—2 Corinthians 5:20 (New International Version)

YOUR TURN

Who are you? Who do you want to BE?

Do your actions come naturally from who you are, or do you define yourself by what you do?

CHAPTER TEN

IS THAT ALL?

We used to practice high school football in August – and boy, was it hot in the Mississippi River Valley of Rock Island. Our team would practice for hours, and we would become incredibly thirsty. We didn't know anything about what athletes should drink so we would drink water or pop. We would drink and drink and drink, but we'd still be thirsty. Pretty soon, all of our stomachs would be bloated but our throats would tell us that we were *still* thirsty. What a terrible feeling.

In trying to quench our thirst, we couldn't stop ourselves. We never did quench it. It's a good example of how no matter what people have, they always seem to want more.

Asking "Is that all there is?" can be helpful, but not as a way to get more stuff. Instead, we can use the question to look beyond material things (and rote habits) and discover what's really important and true.

On our wedding night, Kathy and I prayed, "Lord, take everything out of our lives that is not of you." Now, I'm not saying that He took our money, but he let it dry up. The real estate market went sour and we were really struggling. We prayed more and realized that our financial problems showed us "all there is" beyond wealth. As we recovered, we were grateful for the lessons we'd learned. Our experience forced us to ask, "What else is out there for us?" and helped us feel closer to each other and to Jesus.

That story might scare you. You might be afraid of losing everything – so afraid that you don't look beyond what you have. It's great to be financially comfortable, and to be able to provide for your family and use your wealth to help others in need. But if you're so comfortable that you forget who you are – that is, who you are even without material possessions – then you might need to ask, "What else?" right now.

Let me tell you what else was in store for me – what happened when I opened myself up to the question to see what God had in store for me.

A couple of friends of mine, Curt Weerheim and Scott Mann, asked me to take a basketball team with Athletes in Action to Poland and Greece in the summer of 1990. They were a pretty good team, mostly college athletes, and would play nine games in all. I thought, "I don't know how this works," and I almost declined. I loved coaching, but I'd been focused on regaining what I'd lost in the real estate market. They finally talked me into it. I went on faith, raising $3,300 from friends to fund the trip. This led to a full-time position with Athletes in Action, which changed my life in amazing ways, including the opportunity to create Basketball Club International and the BCI Edge team.

Suddenly, I found myself serving the Lord and doing it as a career. It has been a wonderful journey, but it took faith and it took my looking beyond what I could "get" to make it happen. Winning doesn't make the thirst go away. I had to look at what I could give instead. And in redefining what it means to be satisfied, I found I wasn't thirsty anymore.

First guy: “How can I find God?”

Second guy: “How badly do you want to find Him?”

First guy: “I don’t know.”

So the second guy takes the first guy down to a river and holds his head under the water. Finally, he releases him and asks:

“What did you want when you were under water?”

First guy: “I needed air.”

Second guy: “What would you have done to get air?”

First guy: “I would have done anything to get it.”

Second guy: “That’s how badly you should be thirsting after God. If you want God as much as you wanted air just now, you’ll find Him.”

Everyone who drinks this water will get thirsty again and again. Anyone who drinks the water I give will never thirst – not ever. The water I give will be an artesian spring within, gushing fountains of endless life.

—John 4:13-14 (The Message)

YOUR TURN

How much "stuff" do you really need?

What would it mean to you if you had deeper love? Deeper faith? A deeper commitment to your family? To helping others?

What are you thirsty for in your life? Make a list of the first things that come to mind.

Now, what would *really* quench your thirst? Take your time with this question.

CHAPTER ELEVEN

VIEW FROM THE BRIDGE

I didn't have much money as a student at the University of Iowa, especially for dating. Nobody had cars at school in those days. Luckily, the most romantic place on campus was free and nearby – a railroad bridge over the Iowa River, serving the CRANDIC line (Cedar Rapids and Iowa City). Couples would meet there for conversation and a cheap date – watching the water below from a narrow railroad bridge. If we'd already talked enough about classes, family and sports, we could talk about the fascinating river below.

After spending a lot of time on that bridge, I began really thinking about the experience of the river. I'd go there by myself, just to think and reflect on life. What I came to understand about the river became a significant influence on my inner life and a topic for many of the talks I gave later as a coach and mentor.

A bridge has three basic views – upstream, downstream, or straight down. When you look downstream, you see the water flowing away from you. When you look upstream, you see the water moving toward you. Sometimes it carries branches, leaves, logs or even trash. Straight down, the river can look almost still for a moment. This view from the bridge is just like the view from a well-lived life.

You can't do anything about what's already passed you by. It's gone, for better or worse. Trying to change or reframe the past is futile. But if you look upstream and pay attention to what's coming toward you, you can make a difference. You can keep an eye on the debris as it travels, gets stuck and frees itself. You can duck or push through the obstacles, even if you can't always control what comes down the river. You can prepare yourself, planning your reaction in advance according to your personal values and ambitions.

The view straight down – the present moment – is where the action (and reaction) happens. If you've been paying attention to the events upstream, you can handle the present with integrity and effectiveness. You can also make sure that your own life isn't flowing trash or debris into someone else's river.

I'm reminded of Connie Hawkins, a basketball phenomenon who experienced one of the worst professional setbacks imaginable and finally recovered. He showed outstanding character, patience and work ethic during a situation with a "view" that would level most – unsubstantiated charges of participation in game-fixing and expulsion from a future in the NBA.

Connie was recognized as a serious star in high school, where he played forward in a poverty-stricken urban setting in Brooklyn, N.Y. He was one of six children being raised by an ill, and eventually blind, single mother. Of course, no one in those days expected him to read or even go to class – they just wanted him on the court, scoring points. Connie wasn't able to get a driver's license, but he was courted by many colleges, including the University of Iowa. With the help of Connie's coach at Boy's High School in Brooklyn, Mickey Fisher, I was able to persuade Connie to come to Iowa as a freshman in 1960.

But before Connie could get to Iowa, a charismatic lawyer and businessman approached him and some friends at a playground court, claiming to be a big fan of basketball. The man lent his car to the boys, paid for meals, and even "hired" the boys to play in benefit games he'd organized. To Connie and his Brooklyn friends, the guy and his cronies were just fans who liked to hang out with cool young players. Connie got a few hundred dollars to introduce the men to college players.

While at Iowa, in April 1961, Connie was suddenly taken back to New York to help detectives with their investigation of these men and the gambling ring they were running. The detectives kept him in isolation for more than two weeks, where they interrogated him harshly and, as we understand now, coerced false confessions out of him regarding this gambling ring.

The truth was that Connie didn't know about score-fixing and gambling. He'd never been warned about the scandals of previous decades. He'd already chosen Iowa, and he wasn't playing yet, so he wasn't worried about anyone trying to bribe or manipulate him. He didn't even introduce the players listed in his charges – he didn't have enough clout yet. He was simply a young, poor victim of a really slick, convincing predator. But after a grand jury heard the case, and despite no mention of Connie Hawkins in any formal charges, the NBA smelled a scandal. He was ruled ineligible to play because of an NCAA rule regarding players under investigation. As a result, Connie lost his scholarship and had no choice but to withdraw from the University of Iowa that spring.

I was heartbroken for him. He hadn't been allowed to call me – his coach – or even his own mother as he went through this terrible experience. A few years later, when he'd found work with the Harlem Globetrotters, he said, "One of my biggest regrets is that I didn't get to play for Sharm Scheuerman." I regret, too, that "The Hawk" didn't get to be a Hawkeye.

Connie Hawkins rejected the "revenge" idea and held his head up, despite the pain and discouragement he felt about his reputation and professional potential. He continued to take care of his mother, his wife, and his children by landing a low-paying job with the American Basketball League (who investigated Connie's past and found no evidence of wrongdoing), followed by playing with the Harlem Globetrotters and the Pittsburgh Pipers. Behind the scenes, a lawyer named Dave Littman, whose brother owned the Rens (another Pittsburgh ABL team that employed Connie), had taken a keen interest in Connie's situation. He spent more than 10,000 hours over eight years working to reveal the truth about Connie's situation and to get the NBA to reconsider its position. Eventually, an interrogator admitted he'd coerced the false confessions from the college freshman – but said the tactics were necessary. The head gambler even admitted, after he'd left jail, that Connie had never figured into any fix or attempted fix.

Littman's perseverance – along with Connie's patience and incredible attitude – eventually paid off. In 1969, Connie was finally allowed into the NBA. He joined the Phoenix Suns with a contract that, at the time, was one of the biggest sports deals ever negotiated. It included a signing bonus, a guaranteed five-year salary, and a prepaid annuity for his retirement. Connie was grateful and relieved – for his restored reputation, for his family's new success, and for his own abilities, which would finally be given an NBA venue.

Wilt Chamberlain had said about Connie, "He's the only guy in the world who can completely palm the ball. He can do anything. The Hawk is one of the best three ballplayers I ever saw." And he really, really was.

Connie's view had looked pretty bleak for a while. They say being wrongfully accused or convicted is one of the most devastating things that can happen to a man. But for a long time he couldn't do much about that except to somehow find a way to play anyway. He let good people help him and look out for him. He didn't let anyone think he was destroyed by his experience. He didn't forget to keep looking forward and thinking about what's next – what's coming down the river. And finally, he accepted the (lucrative) invitation to join the NBA and put his past behind him.

As you watch the water pass you by, on a real bridge or just in your imagination, you might wonder what this view will mean to you in the long run, once all of the water has passed under your feet. No matter how difficult things have been for you, or are for you now, remember this: with patience and faith, your view can be truly inspiring in the end.

I often end my letters and e-mails with the salutation, "Looking up." From your view from a bridge, remember what's available to you from that direction, too.

All things work together for good for those who love the Lord and are called according to His purpose.

—Romans 8:28 (New International Version)

YOUR TURN

What has happened in your past that you've had trouble putting behind you?

What can you do right now to cope or correct something about the situation?

What opportunities may be on the horizon? Are you "looking up" too?

CHAPTER TWELVE

JUDGMENT CALL

In 1961, I came awfully close to taking a swing at a lifelong friend. The Hawkeyes had been looking at a strong season, but then we lost four top players because of eligibility problems. So, as head coach, I was elated during our game against Ohio State – the #1 ranked team that included All-Americans Jerry Lucas and John Havlicek – when it looked like we actually had them beat. Our team played over their heads. When we lost in the last few seconds by just one point, I believed we would have won if we'd had our four missing players.

This was enough to put me in a bad mood, but what happened next made it a lot worse. An old friend, an OSU grad, approached me as I walked with my team to our locker room. He happily waved his alma mater's flag at me, right near my face. Hitting him for that would have been the stupidest thing in the world.

My friend didn't know how low I was feeling after that failed high. Most people were patting me on the back and saying, "Great effort," and "Good game." When that flag waved just about right in my face, I had such a strong emotional reaction. What I wanted in the moment (to make him stop) conflicted with what I wanted to have in my life (friends, integrity, compassion). I'm not saying I weighed all of these things in the heat of the moment and made the wise choice. That's not how things usually work. But I was old enough to know it takes only a second to make a bad decision you'll have to live with for a long time. And when you accept that, you've gained a little bit of self control.

Luckily, I was able to head straight down the concourse with my team and address the devastated Hawkeyes as their leader. If I'd hit my friend, it would have been a completely different situation. A good leader has to be less self-centered and focus on his team. You have to set a good example. It's part of earning respect.

The scenario of a professional athlete making a bad decision and quickly or eventually wrecking his reputation and career has become pretty familiar. The media seem to love these stories, but they usually skip the lesson we could be learning from them.

I dealt with a situation recently that involved a couple of players on tour with BCI Edge in Amsterdam for the Haarlem Christmas Tournament. A couple of local gals worked their way into players' rooms. While the players insisted that nothing inappropriate happened, in-room socializing was against BCI rules and incredibly disrespectful to the team, the sponsors, and our international hosts. "Inappropriate" behavior happened the moment they decided to continue their conversation upstairs. The decision was probably made just like that – in a single moment. It was a pretty bad one, considering that they placed their ability to play professional basketball on this tour and for this organization in jeopardy.

A third player discovered the situation and left the room, not telling anyone else at first because he "didn't want to snitch." The truth is, without the rest of the team and the coaches holding these guys accountable for their bad judgment call, the integrity of both the players and the entire trip was at stake. We all need incentive to do what we know is right – and to *not* do what we know will mess things up. Part of the incentive has got to be internal: you want to feel good about yourself and your decisions. You want to feel connected to your values and your faith. And part of it needs to be external: you want to be respected by your peers, fans and leaders. You are a role model and you want to deserve that honor.

I don't like the word "snitch." If your friend or teammate makes a decision to behave in a way that could end his career, ruin his reputation, devastate his marriage, or otherwise cause huge life problems, you've got to talk firmly to him. And you'll probably need reinforcements. I'm not saying you should call the press. Just get other trusted friends involved who are concerned about the well being of this individual. Together, you can hold your buddy accountable for his actions and let him know what it could cost him and why it needs to stop. If he's mad, tell him that's *tough luck*. You step up because you care. He'd better do the same for you.

Every organization and institution has rules. The truth is that if you want to play for someone, you also have to "play ball." I've had a lot of experience working within rules – as a student athlete, a coach, a sports commentator, a real estate developer, a husband, a father, a mentor, and a Christian. The best rules challenge you to be your personal best. For me, my decision to let Jesus live in me was not made in one moment – it happened in many moments over time. And when I let Him come in and take control, I found I could be the man who could look any flag-waving Ohio State friend in the eye and growl, without missing a beat, "We'll get you next time."

But if and when I do make a mistake, I've got good friends who will call me on it. I've also got the Lord to forgive me and help me earn forgiveness from anyone I've affected. There are consequences to every decision you or I make. We owe it to ourselves to take that concept seriously and not think we're immune to the impact of our actions. No one is above the law of cause and effect.

The next time you find yourself at a crossroads, see whether you can predict the possible outcomes – for better or worse – to your next move. If there's no time for that, and you're caught in a heated moment, then do what feels right. By "right," I mean by the rules you've accepted of your profession, your relationships, and your faith. I mean doing what it takes to be the role model and leader you want to be. Plus, it's such a relief to look back and say, "Thank God I didn't do something stupid."

I can make it through anything in the One who makes me who I am.

—Philippians 4:13 (The Message)

YOUR TURN

What rules have you agreed to follow, whether directly (a promise) or indirectly (an understanding)?

What are your personal rules?

Who holds you accountable when you make a bad call?

How do you react when someone calls you out?

CHAPTER THIRTEEN

TAKING IT PERSONALLY

On my first trip with AIA as a coach, we played four games in Poland before heading down to play against teams in the Greek league. In Athens, we stayed at a kind of seminary or monastery that included a Christian school. On one of our days off, the players were off sightseeing and I spent a few hours with the school's headmaster. He happened to be the foremost Christian history teacher in Greece. I enjoyed hearing about Alexander the Great and the Greek elements of the Bible. It was a fascinating conversation and I was in great spirits.

Around 5 o'clock, the guys returned from their tour and we sat down together for some "team talk" time. But suddenly, something hit me emotionally. I said, "Excuse me, I need to run upstairs," and I did run. It felt as if someone had just taken a big water hose and put it at the top of my head and turned it on. It just flushed over my head, flushed me out, scraped out the inside of my head, and even seemed to take away my whole life for a minute. I was crying hard.

It was a little while before I could go back downstairs. I'm not sure I even told the guys how big this was. I may have shared that I'd had a sensation – an experience – I couldn't quite describe but that I think was the Holy Spirit, moving through me like gangbusters.

When I returned to the U.S., I told Kathy that it might have been the most meaningful month of my life so far. Of course, now that I look back over a lifetime, I remember many experiences that moved me, shifted me, surprised me, and even flushed me out. You can't predict these things, but they all have something in common: every experience has been personal, between the Lord and me.

The idea of being "born again" can sound funny to people who don't understand what it really means. Here's how I see it: God can handle only perfection. He's got to change us from our cruddy old selves into new creatures – and the way he did it was to let His son, Jesus, die on the cross for our sins. He paid for our sins so we could all be new creatures, perfect in God's eyes. And if you believe in God, you've got to be grateful that you get to be here on Earth, having been crucified with His son. If you believe, you can be born again – that is, acknowledging that you have been crucified with Christ and that it's no longer you who live but Christ who lives in you. See, Jesus already died for you. All you have to do is accept the gift of His grace.

I remember going to a sermon at an organized church as a young man, a church where a lot of people really liked to be *seen* while they worshiped. I'd never had the Holy Spirit explained to me before, and so when the pastor started reading scripture from the book of John, I paid attention. Then he stopped reading right before the part about the Holy Spirit – the part about the personal relationship. When I asked him about it later, he told me he had some doubts about that part – about the personal relationship. I said, respectfully, "But this is God's word and I don't think we're smart enough to know what to accept and what not to accept." Eventually, I found a church where they talked about the relationship I craved.

Some people think that if I say I live for Him, and accept what He says as truth, that must mean I stand on a street corner with my hands folded, looking at the sky. Or that I can't ever make a mistake. I can tell you neither is true. This isn't about religion; it's a relationship. And prayer is not a one-way conversation.

I live my life. I mess up. But because I live by faith (and yes, wonder "What would Jesus do?" when I'm stumped), I keep going and keep trying my best. There's no giving up. We're in this together.

You may be just starting to think seriously about your spiritual life, or you may be well on your way to a lifelong relationship with Jesus. You might have a spark of *something* in your heart, but haven't ever had an opportunity to ask questions. Wherever you are, consider this:

When we seek His face in worship, it warms His heart.

I have been crucified with Christ and I no longer live, but Christ lives in me. The life I live in the body, I live by faith in the Son of God, who loved me and gave himself for me.

—Galatians 2:20 (New International Version)

YOUR TURN

What are your most important personal relationships?

How do you honor those relationships?

What would you do to deepen your relationship with Jesus?

▲ 1938, Sharm (left) and brother, Tom.

▲ 1938

▲ 1950, Sharm (left) and brother, Tom, with their mother, Lois.

▲ 1951, The Rock Island High School "Rocks," junior year. Sharm Scheuerman, #31, guard.

▲ 1952, Playing with the Rock Island Rocks, senior year.

▲ 1956, Sharm's player card from the University of Iowa.

▲ The original "Fab"ulous Five, University of Iowa Hawkeyes. (left to right) Sharm, Bill Logan, Carl Cain, Coach Bucky O'Connor, Bill Schoof, Bill Seaberg.

▼ Sharm (right) and Bill Seaberg, Hawkeye guards.

▼ 1956, NCAA Championship game. Sharm (#46) going for a layup against Bill Russell of the San Francisco Dons.

MICHIGAN STATE
VS
UNIVERSITY OF IOWA

Jenison Fieldhouse | Saturday, February 19, 1955

EXPERIENCED HAWKEYES

Guard MILT SCHEUERMAN, left, has been a valuable play-maker for the Iowa Hawkeyes this season, picking up where he left off a year ago. He is a 6-2 junior and averages ten points per game. On the right, center BILL LOGAN passes off to forward CARL (Sugar) CAIN in setting up a scoring play for the Iowa five. Logan and Cain, like Scheuerman, made the varsity team a year ago as sophomores.

SPARTAN BASKETBALL NEWS

Price 15c

▲ 1955, Sports Basketball News.

▲ Chasing the ball at Iowa, photo by L. Roger Turner.

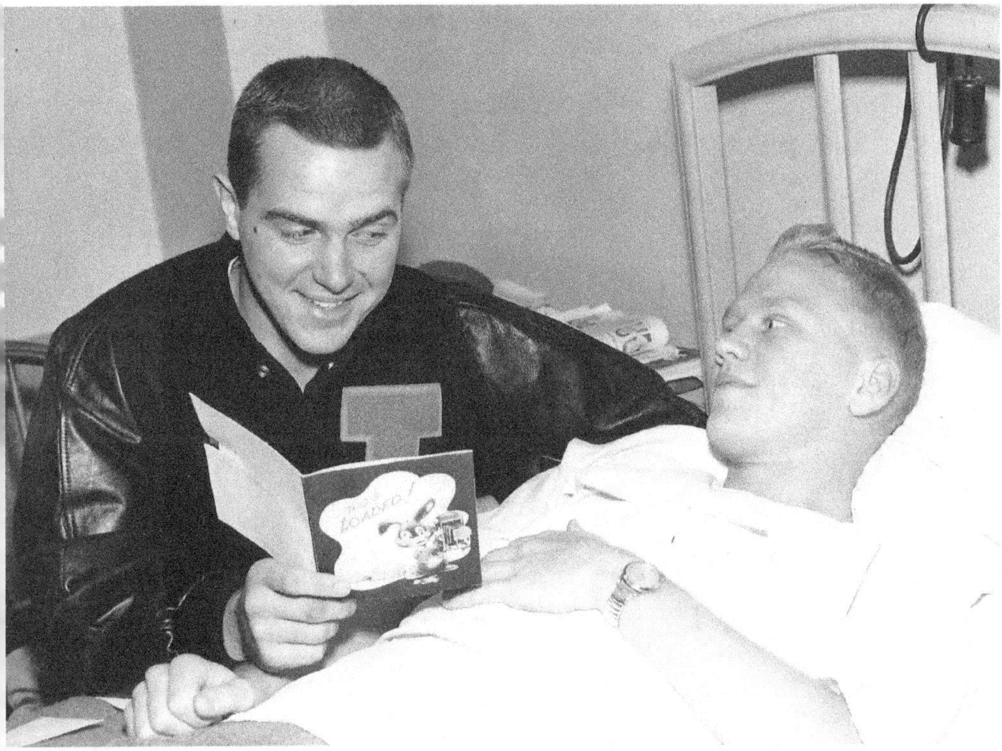

▲ 1955, Sharm blows a kidney playing touch football before the basketball season starts. He's back on the court to start game nine against Ohio State!

▲ 1962, Coach Sharm (left) and Hawkeye Don Nelson. Don "Nellie" Nelson went on to a long career as an NBA player and coach, and was the winningest coach in the NBA.

▲ Coach Sharm, just appointed. The press stopped by to stage photos.

▲Coaching at the University of Iowa.

▲Coach Sharm, in an interview with radio announcer Tait Cummins.

◀1961-1962 University of Iowa Hawkeyes program schedule. Co-captains Joel Novak and Don Nelson with Coach Sharm. Inscription: "Mom – Thought you'd like one just off the press. Much love, Sharm."

▼1961, The "Hustlin' Hawkeyes" with Coach Sharm.

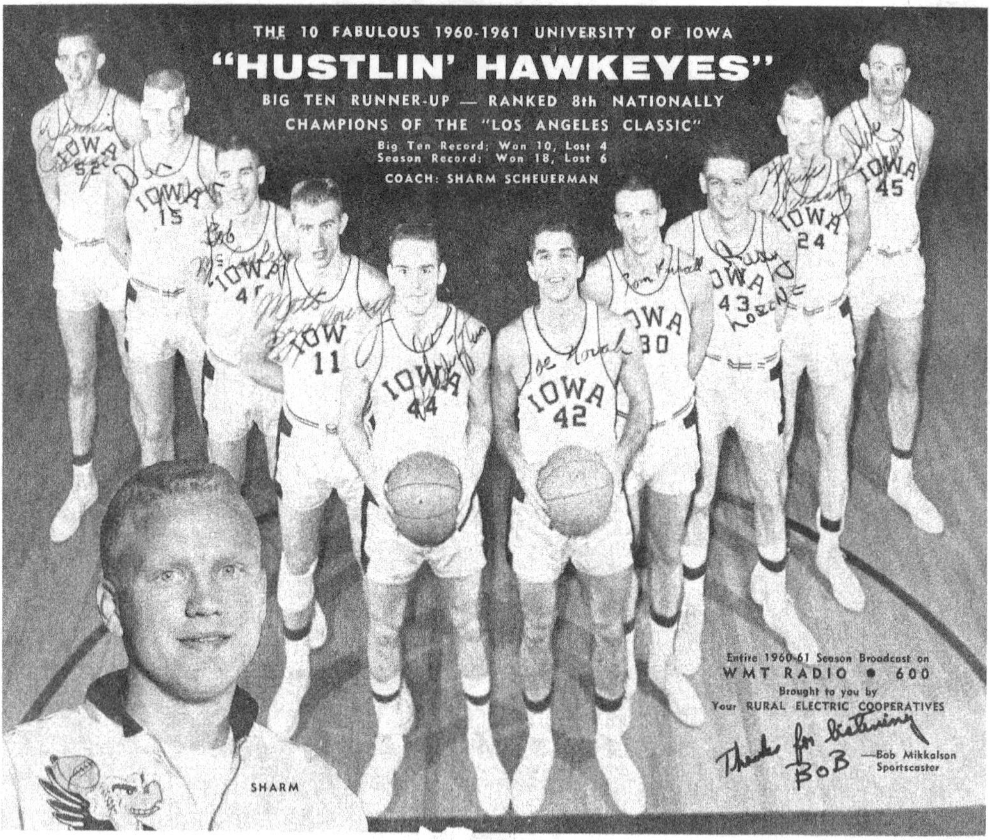

THE 10 FABULOUS 1960-1961 UNIVERSITY OF IOWA

"HUSTLIN' HAWKEYES"

BIG TEN RUNNER-UP — RANKED 8th NATIONALLY

CHAMPIONS OF THE "LOS ANGELES CLASSIC"

Big Ten Record: Won 10, Lost 4
Season Record: Won 18, Lost 6

COACH: SHARM SCHEUERMAN

SHARM

Entire 1960-61 Season Broadcast on
WMT RADIO • 600
Brought to you by
Your RURAL ELECTRIC COOPERATIVES

—Bob Mikkalson
Sportscaster

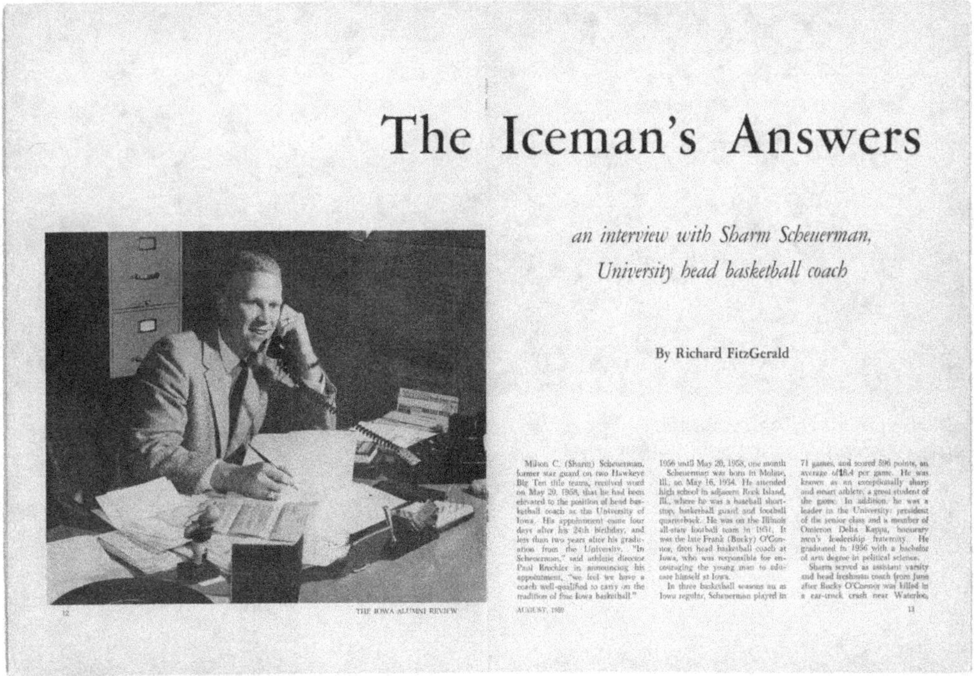

The Iceman's Answers

an interview with Sharm Scheuerman, University head basketball coach

By Richard FitzGerald

Milton C. (Sharm) Scheuerman, former star guard on two Hawkeye Big Ten title teams, received word on May 20, 1958, that he had been elevated to the position of head basketball coach at the University of Iowa. His appointment came four days after his 24th birthday, and less than two years after his graduation from the University. "In Scheuerman," said athletic director Paul Brechler in announcing his appointment, "we feel we have a coach well-qualified to carry on the tradition of fine Iowa basketball."

1956 until May 20, 1958, one month

Scheuerman was born in Moline, Ill., on May 16, 1934. He attended high school in adjacent Rock Island, Ill., where he was a baseball shortstop, basketball guard and football quarterback. He was on the Illinois all-state football team in 1951. It was the late Frank (Bucky) O'Connor, then head basketball coach at Iowa, who was responsible for encouraging the young man to educate himself at Iowa.

In three basketball seasons as an Iowa regular, Scheuerman played in 71 games, and scored 596 points, an average of 8.4 per game. He was known as an exceptionally sharp and smart athlete, a great student of the game. In addition, he was a leader in the University: president of the senior class and a member of Omicron Delta Kappa, honorary men's leadership fraternity. He graduated in 1956 with a bachelor of arts degree in political science.

Sharm served as assistant varsity and head freshman coach from June after Bucky O'Connor was killed in a car-truck crash near Waterloo,

▲ 1959, Article in the Iowa Alumni Review.

▲ 1961, Coach Sharm (bottom row, second from right) with the "West" team, All-Star Shrine East vs. West game.

Bob Hogue and Sharm Scheuerman called the game live on the statewide Iowa Television Network which reaches a potential market of 2.5 million Iowans.

▲ 1984, Color commentary with Sharm and Bob Hogue on the Iowa Television Network.

▶ 2000, Sharm with Athletes in Action.

▼ 1995, Coach Sharm (back row, second from right) with the USA Men's Pan American Games team.

1995 USA MEN'S PAN AMERICAN GAMES TEAM

Silver Medalists -- Mar del Plata, Argentina

March 19 - 25, 1995

▲ BCI Edge in China, 2005. Coach Sharm with Josh Hall (left) and Jason Faulknor.

◀ 2008, Once a Cub, always a Cub.

▼ ▲ 2006, Sharm with players at Roger Powell's RPJ Camp in Chicago.

▲ 2005, Coach Sharm at an international tournament in Las Vegas with BCI Edge, with team director Jordan Obermann (left) and assistant basketball coach Ali Towfigh (right). Coach Towfigh traveled from Iran to participate!

▲ 2006, Coach Sharm with friends of Basketball Club International George Andrews (left) and Jerry Colangelo (right).

▲ 2006, BCI Edge players John Johnson (with camper) and Glen Whisby at a BCI youth clinic in Los Angeles.

▼ 2006, Reed Rawlings and BCI Edge at the Haarlem Basketball Tournament in Amsterdam.

▲ BCI board member TJ Doyle with kids at a BCI Basketball Plus camp in Philadelphia.

▲ 2002, Coach Sharm and Coach Wooden at the Final Four.

▲ Sharm and Kathy Scheuerman, several months following their wedding, December 26, 1981.

CHAPTER FOURTEEN

TEAM OF BROTHERS

From our freshmen year on the University of Iowa basketball team, the guys and I knew we had a great thing. Bill Logan, Bill Schoof, Carl Cain, Bill Seaberg and I just felt the potential between us, knowing that together we were better than any of us could be individually. Carl once said, “We came together at a time when our skills meshed with the coaching we received. When that happened, we became something special.” The U of Iowa basketball team before our “Fab Five” came on the scene had some pretty good players, including my early hero Kenny Buckles. But they didn’t have what we had: real synergy and Olympic dreams.

The planes we chartered to our games were old, rickety, scary, *retired* DC-3s. These were small planes, too, holding about 22 people. Our pilots were hired from the aeronautical school at Purdue University. One trip, from Ohio State, was especially brutal. Carl Cain, who was often my roommate on trips, was praying. We weren’t normally scared of things like this – we usually just played cards and enjoyed our (typical) victory. But thunderstorms were rolling us back and forth, up and down – it felt as if God was throwing us from one hand to the other. Every guy on that flight felt it: we might crash and we’ll be going down together. A lot of us took the train back home from Chicago, even though the second leg of our flight was already booked. I was one who took the train.

On less treacherous flights, our team had a great time. We won a lot, and that made it fun to just sit around on a plane, playing cards, and feeling as if we were on top of the world. It wouldn't have been as fun if we'd lost all the time. Bill Logan, my roommate for two years at Iowa, and I were pretty good at bridge. Gin rummy and euchre were favorites. I'm not sure when we studied! It was important for us to get along like brothers, on and off the court.

We'd sometimes see a movie the night before our game. The whole team would pile into a theater and, soon enough, management would come by and tell us the rule: "No Negroes on the ground floor." So the group of us, black and white, would stand up and move to the balcony level. Soon enough, management would come by and tell us the second rule: "No whites in the balcony." At that point we were done with their ridiculous rules. Our team was a team and we stuck together. We all sat in the balcony. Period.

You get a sense of camaraderie between athletes in high school and college that sometimes seems to be missing in the NBA. It's as if the higher you get, the more you're on your own. I'd like to make a case for teammates – all kinds, at every level of sports, and even in business. Just be available for support, keeping each other on track to success: for accountability, for keeping everyone's egos and choices in check. If not you, then who?

In high school, my friends were thrilled when I inherited my grandfather's 1941 Chevy. I was a junior and most guys didn't get cars until they were older, so I became the designated driver. When I'd pull up to my house at night, I'd say, "Guys, be quiet." But as soon as I'd get out of the car, they'd honk the horn, just to be obnoxious and embarrass me.

This is to say that teammates can sometimes be annoying, like brothers. But life is more fun when you've got friends who are *like brothers* – friends who have something important in common with you, such as values, faith and commitments. Try to hang on to guys like these.

"Individual commitment to a group effort –
that is what makes a team work."

—Vince Lombardi

YOUR TURN

Who are your best friends? What do you have in common?

When you imagine yourself as a senior citizen, which of your current friends do you see in that picture and why?

CHAPTER FIFTEEN

ICE IN THE VEINS

After a particularly charged game in 1955 in which I'd kept my cool, the press said I must have ice in my veins and they started calling me "The Rock Island Ice Man." The Hawkeyes were playing against the University of Minnesota at their home arena. At the time, it was probably the largest campus arena in the U.S. – and the crowd set a record that night for the biggest ever at a college basketball game on a college campus. Usually, for a crowd like this, we played at a municipal auditorium.

Minnesota had an outstanding team, with guys who would end up playing pro ball. Iowa had finished the previous season at #2 in the Big Ten Championships and we knew we could do a lot better.

I think the score was tied or they were a point ahead of us. The important part is that we were in the last minute of that game and Chuck Mencel, an All-American from Minnesota, was just *holding* the ball at center count.

These days, there's a five-second rule – a player can hold the ball only five seconds before he's gotta pass or it becomes a jump ball. Back then, you could hold the ball for five minutes if you wanted to.

I was closely guarding Chuck. I knew he was better than I was, but I knew I had to get this ball moving. So I started inching out on him a bit and talking to him without moving my lips. The sold out crowd was going nuts. I said, quietly, "Hey, these people don't want to watch you stand here holding the ball. They want you to do something with it." I inched out on him a little more, getting closer and closer.

I said for only his ears, "This is boring for the fans," and knew I was getting inside of his head. He'd have to move. Since he was right-handed, I knew he'd go to his right with the dribble. So, I suddenly made a big fake lunge to my right (his left). Then I jumped left (his right) and played defense. When he charged me, the official made a call on him, like he'd hit me. The crowd was crazy. I could feel their rage. But I had a job to do. I went to the line, made both free throws, and we won the Big Ten Championship by those points.

I loved feeling like outside circumstances couldn't touch me. It was a thrilling experience to be on the court and in charge. My team had played a winning game, and I wasn't about to let some All-American stand there with the ball, waiting out the clock, trying to take that away from us. I was willing to do what needed to be done, and then I got down to the business of sinking those free throws with just seconds left in the game. Today, they call a player like that a "money man."

In a way, my "Iceman" nickname was right on. In another way, though, it wasn't. I wasn't that way in my personal life. I left that on the court. People don't always see what's going on under the surface, inside of a player. I see this a lot with the NBA and professional athletes in my life. It's like they have two lives – one public and one private. They worry about letting the wires cross, and with good reason. The public doesn't always seem interested in knowing what's really behind their hero's high score.

Most athletes are just regular guys who happen to have talent. We have prepared ourselves for challenges just like anyone, but we have to do it both physically and psychologically. Sometimes our coaches help us do it. Vince Lombardi told me that when he coached Jerry Kramer with the Green Bay Packers, he used a special strategy whenever they were getting ready to play against top Detroit Lions guard Alex Karras (also a U. of Iowa alum and, later, a football commentator and actor). On a Wednesday, after two days off, Vince would walk by Kramer and say, "Hey, we've got the Lions on Sunday." That's all he'd say. The next day, Vince would offer, "You're going to be against Karras." On Friday, he'd say, "I've been watching films on Karras … not sure you can handle him." Jerry later said that Vince would have him so fired up to play against Karras on Sunday that he was "sky high."

No one can be "up" all of the time. Even the best players have to choose which games and which plays will get 100% and which will get less. When you play lesser teams, for example, sometimes you aren't as intense. But no matter who you're playing, some things have to stay consistent. It's still you, and your reputation, on the court. It's still your team that needs you. And underneath the bravado, it's still the real *you* that has to deal with the aftermath of the game and the fallout from your life choices. Nobody, after all, is made of ice.

"Don't let outside circumstances affect you; you affect outside circumstances"

—Me

YOUR TURN

Are you cool under pressure?

How do you psych yourself up for a challenge?

Can you remove your "game face" when the game is over? This could apply to athletics, school, or anywhere else you feel you adopt a "game" persona to achieve success.

CHAPTER SIXTEEN

INVINCIBLE

A lot of NBA players will get room service on the road, avoiding public recognition and even other players as much as possible. It's not like college, where half the team goes out to eat together the night before each game. These pro players are so bombarded with people all the time; it's understandable that they'd want a little privacy. The problem is that it can turn into isolation. When you're talented and alone, you start to think you're extra-powerful and that whatever you do is just fine.

It seems to start in middle school, where the kids with great talent are shown – by the example set by adults around them – that little they do off the court matters. They think that as long as they play very, very well, someone will take care of them. If their grades aren't good, it will be handled. If they get in trouble with a girl, it will be handled. I know pro players who were given this treatment for years, and now they're suffering, because they never learned how to take personal responsibility. As big and physically strong as they are, they didn't grow up to be mentally and spiritually strong, independent men.

I see young men who look up to professional athletes also adopt this attitude because "invincibility" seems like a lot of fun. The "Who cares?" attitude has become a big problem for kids and their heroes today. When a top athlete messes up, the public relations machine starts spinning excuses. It seems popular to enter rehab for just about *anything*.

Now, instinctively, we all know we're not invincible. You can't throw a white tennis ball against a dirty wall long before it starts getting dirty and dirtier. Pretty soon, "Who cares?" doesn't look so cool. It just looks lazy and pathetic. You can't fix that in rehab.

The truth is, we're all fragile – like my Hawkeyes felt flying on those ancient DC-3s. Our physical and mental lives are absolutely temporary – just wisps of smoke that appear for a little while and then vanish. And while we're here, we've got the opportunity to do a few amazing things: live a life according to our own values and beliefs, and address life's most urgent question, according to Martin Luther King Jr., "What are you doing for others?"

For me, the opportunity to feel truly alive – and both powerful and fallible – came when I let Jesus live in my heart at a later age. I was a kid like many kids: confident in my youthful abilities, full of big plans, and raised by parents who believed in God but didn't quite explain what I needed to know.

I think a lot of young people procrastinate about their own spirituality. I know I did. I always thought, "There's gotta be a lot more to this than I understand. I'll need to look into that later." By the time I started to take a serious look at a personal relationship with Jesus, I realized I'd been on the path for a long time – and little by little, I'd gotten to a point where I was finally ready. I'd been searching all along.

Do you know what faith is? "It's the assurance of things hoped for. It's the conviction of things not seen," (Hebrews 12). We can't see the wind, but we can sure feel the effects of it. We had terrific winds in Denver the other day. It knocked down trees and did much damage. It was the top story on the news. That's what faith is: counting on the effect – and with full assurance that what you hope for is true.

And if you have faith, you don't need to fool yourself into feeling invincible. You can stop focusing on yourself and, instead, think of how you can make an impact in the *real* world. Whoever you are, you're running out of time.

> *Yet you do not know what your life will be like tomorrow. You are just a vapor that appears for a little while and then vanishes away.*
>
> —James 4:14 (New American Standard)

YOUR TURN

Do you ever catch yourself saying, "Who cares?" out loud or just to yourself? Is the statement really true – or do you mean something else by it?

What would you do *for others* if you knew you could not fail?

CHAPTER SEVENTEEN

WHO ARE YOU?

When it was time for me to declare a major at the University of Iowa, I chose business. It seemed like an obvious, versatile choice for an athlete. Then I took an accounting class and ended up misplacing seven cents in my balance sheet on a big project exam. I looked and looked. I ended up getting so frustrated with that missing seven cents that I decided this major would drive me crazy. I switched to political science.

When young, we look at choices like which sport, which college and which major as defining moments in life. We think answering these questions (along with later questions such as "Should I marry this cute girl?") will help define us to ourselves and to others. We think it'll help answer the question, "Who am I, really?"

It doesn't.

Sure, these are all big decisions. Life-changers. Worthy of serious thought and good advice. But the question of who you are isn't about the big decisions. It's about the person you choose to be every day, within the frame of whatever athletic, educational, professional or relationship direction you've taken. That's where significance comes from.

In an earlier chapter, I talked about the BE attitude, where, if you first decide to be your best, you'll naturally do things to support that. If you start with the doing, instead of the being, you might achieve success without significance. You'd find out pretty quickly that success doesn't feel the way you thought it would. As Bob Buford says in his great book *Halftime*, some people start focusing on their own significance – what they contribute to the world – in the second half of their life. It's never too early to start, though.

Carl Cain, my Hawkeye teammate who remains a close friend to this day, always said, "When people show you who they are, believe them."

I like to think that I show people who I am pretty clearly these days. Being 76 years old and still surrounded by young basketball players, from middle school to the professional level, I need to answer the question, "Who am I?" all the time. I have lots of answers, all about *being*. And when it comes to my faith, I'm not ashamed to talk about it in front of anyone.

I'm Sharm Scheuerman. I want to identify myself with Jesus. I'm committed to glorifying God on earth and accomplishing the work He's sent me here to do. I'm committed to taking pro-level basketball to higher grounds with Basketball Club International, encouraging a new kind of sports hero. I'm committed to my wife, Kathy. I'm committed to sticking around as long as He'll let me, for the family and friends I love, the players and kids I mentor, and the BCI organization I'm growing. I am content in the life I lead now, and in the life I've led, because "who I am" is all about the journey. Faith, really, is the journey.

He who began a good work in you will continue to perfect it until the day of Christ Jesus.

—Philippians 1:6 (New International Version)

YOUR TURN

Who are you? Does it align with who others think you are?

How have your ideas about who you are changed over time?

When you're 76 years old, who do you hope to be?

CHAPTER EIGHTEEN

RUNNING AWAY

I ran away two times in my life. The first time, I was 5 years old, mad as I could be, and probably just wanted someone to follow me. I got about 10 blocks from home before I turned around and saw no one was coming after me. The second time was in my sophomore year at the University of Iowa. This time I ran home to my mother in Rock Island with the intention of quitting the basketball team I loved.

In a game against Ohio State, I went 0-0-5. That means no field goals, no free throws, and five fouls. I'd fouled out. I said, "If I can't play better than that, I'm leaving the team." I just about convinced myself that quitting my team was the best thing I could do for everybody counting on me. I rationalized that it wasn't a selfish move; it was *selfless*!

I showed up at home and had to face my mother. She wasn't expecting me, but she got a call shortly from coach Bucky O'Connor. Those two started working on me. Mom said, "You can't just quit. This is not the way you've been brought up." Bucky said, "Sharm, it was one bad game. Come back." But I was incredibly despondent. I said, "I can't go back." I thought, "I don't want to embarrass my team any more by letting my teammates down."

Mom was always Mom. She knew me and knew I'd go back. Bucky did, too. I'm sure he'd seen this kind of thing before. I don't know if it was bravado or what, but after about 24 hours, I got over myself and went back to Iowa. I never had an experience like that again, where I felt like things were so bad that I needed to get out of there ASAP. I *decided* to never let that happen again.

That season ended up being a great one for me and for our team. I can't imagine how horrible it would have felt to miss it. I was lucky that my little detour didn't last longer. A lot of times in life, when you quit something, that's it. No U-turns. A decision you make to walk away, in a split second, can be a decision you'll regret forever.

Running away because you're afraid you don't measure up is just selfish. Running away because you want someone to fetch you and boost your ego is selfish. Either way, it's all about "me, me, me." I imagine every kid in the world runs away for similar reasons. I remember calling to my daughter, Jamey, as she would walk down the street, running away from home. "Bye Jamey, let us know how you're doing!" It was a game to her. But sometimes adults do it, too, even though they know better. And then it's no game.

Part of being a hero is taking your own ego out of the equation and just doing the work that needs to be done. My dad taught my brother, Tom, and me that you should always work more than what you get paid for. Just keep doing your best and keep improving.

And if you ever feel so terrible that you think everyone would be better off if you suddenly quit – your job, your team, your marriage, or anything else – think again. If you really need to change a situation, there are more honorable and thoughtful ways to do it.

As the old saying goes:
"A winner never quits and a quitter never wins."

YOUR TURN

Have you ever walked out on a situation and regretted it?

How would you counsel a friend who has suddenly quit his team? His job? His marriage?

CHAPTER NINETEEN

WHICH WAY IS UP?

Security is often just an illusion – a slippery little railing that you think will keep you from falling. We've got one on our deck in Denver, 21 floors above street level. Holding the railing, I can stand looking straight down and it won't bother me a bit. If it weren't for the railing – that illusion of safety – I guarantee I'd go straight down.

So can the decisions you make in life keep you from misfortune or even disaster? Can you find real security?

Yes and no.

Younger men often ask me, "How do I know I'm on the right path in life?" First of all, you can start with the things you shouldn't be doing. And if there are a few areas of improvement you could really hang your hat on, I'd start there. Notice what would make you feel uncomfortable to reveal to your mother or your coach. If the choices you make would be appropriate to make in front of a room full of people who respect you – or even look up to you – then it's probably OK.

If you're already more spiritual, I'd advise you – emphatically – to begin with prayer. Then start thinking about the pros and cons of the decisions currently in front of you. What are the advantages? What are the negatives? What are your desires?

Note: If you're trying to make a decision about a girl, don't show her these lists.

Consider the potential consequences for every decision you make. If you make good decisions, the outcome will probably be pretty good. A good decision is one that benefits many more people than it would hurt. It doesn't necessarily have to be all about you.

While I was recruiting players for the University of Iowa, I'd counsel them about their decision-making process. "Pick out three schools you think you'd be happy attending," I'd say. "If you can identify three, then you can be happy wherever you go. There won't be a wrong choice. Don't worry or have second thoughts. Just go with your gut." These days, instead of "Go with your gut," I say, "Pray about it." It's more effective.

It concerns me when people making a decision say, "Wish me luck" or "I'll just hope for the best." To me, hope is an assurance guaranteed by a grantor. If someone says, "I hope I make the right choice," what they're really saying is that they wish for it. Hope without a grantor, without Jesus, is just a wish. And wishes can leave you feeling pretty empty and disappointed – and just as paralyzed with indecision as you were before.

So, if you're choosing between three alternatives you already feel good about, you're in good shape. But if you're looking at a choice that you know could be a bad one, you're also looking at some consequences that you'll regret. And all the wishing in the world isn't going to change that.

One of the worst decisions I've ever made – and definitely the dumbest thing I've ever done in business – cost me half a million dollars. In the late '70s, some partners and I were developing a piece of beautiful land near Genesee, Colo. We sold the lots to a builder on a three-year contract, and I went to my bank and borrowed on that contract. Then, interest rates skyrocketed to about 20%. That meant no buyers for the lots. Our builder went bankrupt and I had to sell my contract at a serious discount. First lesson learned: never borrow against a contract, even though it may appear solid. Second lesson learned: don't count on something that doesn't deserve my hope and faith.

I thought that land contract was my security – pretty dangerous thinking. You could have the most lucrative contract in NBA history, but you could mess it up. Someone else could mess it up for you. A lot of guys think, "Now I've got the contract, my work is done. Just gotta hang on to that contract." But the truth is that you may never be "all set."

It's great to make a living doing what you love. If you can achieve financial stability that way, you're lucky. But if you really want to be practical about security, take the financial part out of the equation. No matter how wealthy and powerful, or how poor and powerless you may become, these things are temporary. No promise, on paper or from the mouth of a person you trust, can be 100% secure. Uncertainty is just part of life in this world.

Before I really got the concept of finding real security in Jesus, my life wasn't terrible, but it was a bit of an illusion. Looking back, I'm not comfortable with the idea of trusting an illusion. Now I think that situations like my Genesee experience were God's way of getting my attention. It's like He was saying, "You've got to look up to know which way 'up' is."

"Ask and it will be given to you; seek and you will find; knock and the door will be opened to you."

—Matthew 7:7 (New International Version)

YOUR TURN

Have you thought about praying when faced with a tough decision?

Has something gone terribly wrong for you? How did your choices factor into the outcome? What lesson did you learn?

Where's your security? What's illusion? What's real?

CHAPTER TWENTY

WOMEN & MEN

My mom was the greatest, most loving, and most thoughtful person I've ever known. She was also humble. I like to think I've got a lot of my mom's characteristics, but I feel as if I'm not being humble when I say that. Also, I don't want to sound too proud of being humble!

My father passed away when I was in ninth grade, and his friends would say, "Sharm, you have to be the man of the household." I took it to heart. Without anyone saying more, I determined that there would be nothing I'd do in life that would bring dishonor – or even just a dark cloud – to my mother.

I think many guys feel an enormous love and respect for their mothers or grandmothers – more than they might feel for most others throughout their lives. Often it's the mom (or grandma) who raises the kids by herself, whether due to abandonment or tragedy. Most of us would never dare say something negative about our own mothers. So why do many guys – athletes or not – insult each other's mothers, trying to be funny? Or, they'll say, "son-of-a-b...." without thinking and knowing what that really means.

Many times, kids watch their athlete-heroes treat women terribly. Infidelity, derogatory name-calling and even prostitution are part of the regular news cycle. TV and movies make light of dysfunctional, even abusive marriages (and unwed, cohabitating couples) with a laugh track.

The new "normal" is disturbing, because it's just not loving or respectful. It's certainly not how our mothers taught us to treat women.

My mom asked me for one thing: "Promise me you will not get married until after you graduate from college." But I owed her much more than that. I have always tried to make good decisions regarding women. I haven't been perfect, but I've tried to at least be honest and respectful. Every woman in your life deserves that.

Part of respecting women is realizing that they interpret things differently from the way men do – especially with regard to relationship dynamics. Men need to respect that difference and try to see things from a female perspective. What we see as forgetfulness, they might view as not caring. What we see as a brief lapse in judgment, they might view as a statement about our commitment. And if a guy really gets in trouble and has an affair, however brief, she'll see it as the ultimate betrayal. And she'll be right.

I did wait until after college before marrying Karlen, my first wife. In fact, we married the summer after I graduated. I started on staff at Iowa on June 1, sleeping in Coach Bucky O'Connor's basement through the summer. After Karlen and I got married in August 1956, we found a rental near campus. We bought a house in our second year together – a little bungalow. I'd buy a bunch of six packs and get the guys to come over to paint and help us fix it up. Looking back, it feels like I was very young. Karlen and I had three children together (Tom, Greg, and Jamey) and stayed together until 1975. I met my wife Kathy in 1981 and we're still going strong.

In between my first and second marriages, I enjoyed dating. But I was always conscious of a few things. First, I wanted to be 100% respectful of every woman I met. Second, I knew I had some growing up to do – especially spiritually – before I would get married again. I counsel young men to pray about their decisions regarding who to marry and when. Something as simple as whether someone is a morning or night person can make a difference if you're not careful. I'm glad I waited until I'd matured a bit before I married Kathy. I'll bet she's glad, too.

Do not let any unwholesome talk come out of your mouths, but only what is helpful for building others up according to their needs.

—Ephesians 4:29 (New International Version)

YOUR TURN

What do adults in your life show you (by example) about relationships?

What are the qualities you want to find (or currently have) in your partner? What qualities do you offer?

Do you make jokes about the opposite sex? Why? What does that accomplish?

CHAPTER TWENTY-ONE

INJUSTICE

A classic example of "I was wronged!" comes after a player is thrown out of a basketball game. I've got a few of those stories myself. I was in eighth grade the first time I was thrown out of a game. One of the referees was a math teacher at my junior high school, and he went to church with us. My mom always used the word "shoot" as an expression of her displeasure, so I always used it, too. But when the referee heard me this time, he thought I said something else. I tried to explain, but he called a technical anyway. Waiting until after the game to explain what happened to my dad, well, that was torture. I could see him sitting in the stands, still in his work clothes, watching the game. I was so embarrassed and worried. What would he say about my getting thrown out of the game? Would he believe me? This was back in the day when kids, even teenagers, got their mouths washed out with soap. Plus, what my dad thought of me was very important.

As a junior at Iowa, playing in the NCAA tournament against Morehead State, I got thrown out for retaliating against a bully. Morehead had a lot of veterans returning from the Korean War and they were tough guys. One was not only a tough player, but also a dirty player. He constantly elbowed me away from the ball and gave me cheap shots. The officials didn't see it happening. I kept telling him to lay off, but he wouldn't.

Late in the third quarter, I had the ball and was called for traveling. No question it was the right call. I was mad at myself. But this player came up and grabbed me from the back, like he was going after the ball. Instead, he hit me hard in the back. When I turned and saw who it was – the guy who'd been elbowing me all game – I just went after him. Did I punch him? He backed away real quick, but I know I got him a few times. The official knew it, too, and threw me out of the game.

My first time getting a technical as a coach was against Arizona in Portland, Ore., at a Christmas tournament. You can imagine how exciting it was for Portland basketball fans to watch an afternoon game between Iowa and Arizona. There were probably fewer than 500 people in the stands.

I didn't think one of the officials was doing a good job. He seemed to be listening to comments from the crowd, instead of relying on his own observations. We call that having "rabbit ears." I'd been venting during the whole game, saying things like, "There's no way you could have seen that." But when he happened to turn toward me, I added, "And you've got rabbit ears, too." Well, he didn't like that comment one bit and he threw me out. I wasn't a rant-and-rave kind of coach. I didn't think what I said was that bad. But I went to the locker room and thought, "I don't want to be in here," and subsequently walked back to the hotel.

I'm a big believer in "once it's over, learn from it and move on." I don't see the point in dwelling. You don't often get do-overs, no matter how much you wish for one. And when something happens that you feel isn't right, isn't fair, and maybe even a little embarrassing, then it's not going to do much good to feel sorry for yourself or retaliate.

My cancer's not fair, but it's just the way it is. No cancer is fair. Because of my faith, I don't feel sorry for myself. It's no longer I who live, but Christ who lives in me. I can't just give Him part of my life.

Either He's going to get it all or He'll take nothing. You can't just plug Him into certain chapters of your life. That's not how this works.

So, my life is in His hands. There are days I feel like I'm not going to be around for a while. I'm just taking what's dealt to me and doing my best with it. I still make plans – big plans – and have every intention of following through with them for as long as I can.

In eighth grade, when the math teacher kicked me out of the game, my father believed me. This huge injustice had me in knots – but it didn't turn out to be the crisis I thought it was.

In my junior year, after I got kicked out during our game against Morehead State, my team prepared to play Kentucky the next day. It was the finals of the regional tournament to get to the Final Four. We warmed up and headed back to the locker room to use the bathroom, blow our noses, and get final instructions from Coach O'Connor. After his talk, Coach asked, "Do you guys have any questions?" Our forward, Bill Schoof, who had a great sense of humor, raised his hand and asked, "Are they going to introduce Sharm as the champ or the challenger tonight?" Coach threw up his hands and said, "Get outta here!" I think I had my best scoring of all time that night. I was charged up for a comeback!

After getting kicked out as a coach for the "rabbit ears" comment, I felt embarrassed. I didn't want to talk to the players. I was reminded that I wasn't such a tough, macho guy. If I had been, I might have said something a lot more colorful. I was usually so mild-mannered. But every coach loses it sometimes, because the pressure and responsibility are so great, whether that means saying "rabbit ears" or something actually worth a technical. The players know it's between the coach and the official. They know we're just standing up for them. Good officials will let the coaches vent a little – it's just part of the game.

When you let sourness take over after a disappointment, it's like saying to God, "I don't trust you." It's like you want to believe in Him when things are good. You thank Him. You praise Him. But then when the going gets tough, you say, "I didn't sign up for this! Not fair!"

There's a big difference between questioning and doubting. I ask questions all the time, but I don't doubt Him. For example, I might say, "Lord, I know you're capable of healing the cancer that's in me. I know you can, but it might be that you want to call me home instead. Whatever your reason, I trust you. So what shall I do while I'm still here? How can I continue to serve you?" Legendary UCLA coach John Wooden famously said, "Make each day your masterpiece." It's not always easy, but what else are you going to do? Whine? It's a lesson best learned sooner than later.

"For My thoughts are not your thoughts, neither are your ways My ways," declares the Lord.

—Isaiah 55:8 (New International Version)

YOUR TURN

How you do react when things just don't go your way?

Do you trust that the Lord is paying attention?

What kind of attitude do you think Jesus had before he was crucified? Vengeance? Forgiveness? Trust in His Father?

CHAPTER TWENTY-TWO

ONE CINDERBLOCK SHORT

For my first five years, we lived in an old place down by the Mississippi River. It had a potbelly stove for heat, and my dad had cut holes in the ceiling to heat the floors upstairs. Then he built us a home up on the hill in Rock Island – a small bungalow. But to save money, he dug the basement six feet deep instead of seven: one cinderblock short.

It was a low space, but we set up a basketball net anyway – at around four feet high – and played as much as possible. It was the only place to bounce a basketball in the winter without having to shovel. And when we did shovel, or in the summer when the driveway was clear, we had to play on a severe slope. Our house was built on a six-foot terrace from the street and the driveway dropped six feet down. The farther you got from the basket, the more you shot uphill. Dribbling wasn't so bad, but shooting on an incline throws you off a bit.

While it would have been nice to have a level playing field near the house, and room to play in the basement without hitting our heads, my brother, Tom, and I had a great time. We probably complained a bit, but looking back, I remember only the fun of it. Maybe life isn't as complicated as we sometimes make it out to be.

We had to shovel snow a lot, just to play ball. We had to do chores, just to have some free time. I remember getting a free bicycle from one of my dad's friends but, before I could even ride it, I had to spend hours and hours fixing and cleaning the thing. It built character and taught me there's no such thing as a free lunch.

So, what happened to work?

Kids used to play a bunch of different sports, as many as they could season-to-season, and play for the fun of it. If they were especially talented in a few, they continued to play them in college. Now, kids as young as 9, or even younger, are encouraged to focus on just one sport, and only if they show great talent for it.

If a young athlete happens to show a lot of potential, the pressure begins. The ego starts to get stroked. The free shoes start arriving. The vultures circle.

So, what happened to fun?

Life can and should be a lot of work and a lot of fun. I think – as a society – we've lost some of that, along with a lot our values. It sure is easy to be critical, but I'm also trying to do something about it with BCI and BCI Edge. We're trying to inject some values, integrity, faith, and even some fun into the world of pro basketball and its sphere of influence.

I knew a player for AIA whose father was a minister. We'd be in the locker room between warm-ups and the game, just getting psyched up as a team, and somebody would point out that this player was missing. We'd find him around the corner, reading his Bible. I'd have to say, "There are 24 hours in the day. You don't have to read your Bible all 24 of those hours. Especially when you're getting ready to play a game. You need to focus on basketball right now. So get your tail in here and pay attention!"

So, what happened to balance?

This is my challenge to you: don't be afraid of a little hard work or a little informal play, and remember not to focus on one so much that you forget the other. Don't lose sight of what's important to you. You really don't want to end up *one cinderblock short* of a full life!

I came so they can have real and eternal life, more and better life than they ever dreamed of.

—John 10:10 (The Message)

YOUR TURN

When is the last time you worked really hard for something, and finally watched it pay off?

When is the last time you played, just for fun?

CHAPTER TWENTY-THREE

TOUGH STREET

My grandfather, my mother's father, taught Greek and the Bible at Augustana College in Rock Island for 40 years. My dad built a house for him and my Grandma Suze just a few blocks away from ours. At meals, if my brother or I would act up – or even laugh – our grandfather would begin drumming his fingers on the dining room table. When the fingers started drumming, we knew we'd better shape up quick. He'd look at us with the most penetrating, stern eyes I've ever seen. One look had a gigantic effect on Tom and me.

Grandma Suze, a strict Lutheran, showed some of this severe attitude, too, after my grandfather passed away. She had a pretty good personality, but she didn't always show it. Mom was much more loving and sweet than her parents. But Suze would sometimes get so exasperated with us that she'd say, to our delight, "My name is Tough. I live on Tough Street. The farther down you go, the tougher it gets. And I live in the last house."

When I was at Iowa, we played Purdue in an old armory where the students could sit right under the basket. During our pregame warm-up, the students would come down and get as close as they could on the court and taunt us. It was a tough crowd. In our warm-up drill, the starting five would shoot free throws while the other seven would stand in a circle and pass the ball to warm up. Then we'd switch: seven would shoot free throws while our starting five would pass the ball around. One night, there were a couple of extra loud mouths right in close to us. So fellow starter Bill Schoof (who was also a great pitcher for the U. of Iowa baseball team) said, "We've got to shut them up." He winked at me and then, instead of passing the ball, he wound up throwing the ball at this mouthy kid. Bill was pretty accurate. He said, "Oh, I am so sorry!" We did it just to irritate them as much as they were irritating us. It happened more than once.

Sometimes, you've got to be tough. Even if you don't feel it, you've got to put on the toughest face you can and stand up for yourself and the people you care about.

In March of 1982, I was doing the color commentary for an important Big Ten championship game between Iowa and Purdue. It was a very close game, getting right down to the wire. In the last 12 or 15 seconds, a player took a shot from the corner. I think we were tied because Purdue shot and everyone ran toward the basket. An official under the basket, whose name I won't mention (but he's infamous in Iowa), suddenly called a foul on Iowa at the free throw line. He called it from under the basket, through an impenetrable wall of players.

The fouled player, Kevin Boyle, went nuts. Purdue made one of its two free throws and won the game. Iowa went berserk. We were all in shock.

As a color commentator, my table was a foot and a half below the floor level. I looked up and saw Iowa's coach, Lute Olson, running across the court for the official. I took my headgear off, jumped onto the court, and ran as fast as I could after Lute. Our play-by-play guy was still talking. He didn't even realize I'd taken off!

I was thinking two things. First, "If Lute goes into the officials' locker room, he'll probably lose his job. I've got to stop him." Second,

"If Lute's already in the officials' locker room when I get there, I'm going in there with him."

Kevin Boyle was already in the hallway, banging the wall. We stopped Lute just in time, and he yelled at the officials from outside their locker room. It was an incredibly charged moment – just about out of control. I thought Kevin might have broken his hand on the wall. I had a good sports coat on, but I held him as hard as I could. He was beside himself. Everyone was yelling. I just remember saying, "Calm down. You can't do anything right now. Terrible call, terrible call." You've got to put on your "Tough Street" face for times like that.

That official, by the way, turned up a few hours later in Kansas City to officiate another game. Kathy pointed him out to me on the TV and I did a complete double take. I said, "He can't be in Kansas City. I just saw him at Purdue!" A lot of people in Iowa thought he called the foul on Boyles – on anyone – because he couldn't afford to let the Iowa-Purdue game go into overtime or he would have missed connection for his flight to Kansas City. After some Iowans went overboard in expressing anger over the situation (threats, T-shirts), the Big Ten Conference would no longer allow the man to officiate Iowa games. It was too dangerous to his health.

"When the going gets tough, the tough get going."

—Joseph P. Kennedy

YOUR TURN

When do you put on your "Tough Street" face?

When do you take it off?

CHAPTER TWENTY-FOUR

MAKING THINGS RIGHT

I know a player who, while he knew about Jesus, hadn't committed his life to Him. This player, a McDonald's All-American, got married, had a child, and then a little later had an affair with his wife's sister. His wife left him. When I asked him how things were going, he said, "I don't want a divorce. I love my wife." I told him, "Start by swallowing your pride. If you have any sort of resistance to what she tells you, or if you try to justify anything you've done, it's not going to work. You've got to humble yourself and do what she tells you. You've got to earn her trust and it's going to take a lot of time." The last time I talked to him, things seemed to be moving in a good direction. He has stepped up in his commitment to Jesus, too. I don't think this is a coincidence.

The worse you mess up, the harder it is to make it right. I've seen so many players who feel entitled to behave just about however they want. They think that if they make a mistake, they'll be able to ignore the consequences. Some guys think they're too important to be held accountable. I think the media have shown us, whether we want to see it or not, that no sports star is too big to fail.

So if you really want to make things right after making a mistake, start with acknowledging what you did, accept your responsibility and how it has affected others. Don't be too big to apologize. Don't assume that your role in someone's life gives you a free pass. Forgiveness is earned through hard work more than anything.

Forgiveness by Jesus is another story. Because he was crucified for our sins, we've already been forgiven. This is about grace. Grace is a gift. It's free, and we can do nothing to earn it because Jesus gave it to us a long time ago. One of the things Jesus said on the cross was, "It is finished." That means he paid the price for us. All we have to do is believe and accept it.

That said, we can't just go off the deep end and say, "I'm saved. I believe. Once saved, always saved. Now I've got permission to be as awful/lazy/cruel as I please." People who think that way are headed for trouble. If you really believe and understand grace, then you know that "It is no longer I who live but Christ who lives in me," (Galatians 2:20). If Christ lives in you, then you're compelled to behave in a way that's in line with Him. We're never going to be perfect, and being a goody-goody isn't the point anyway. All we have to do is believe in Him and open up to Him. The good works will follow automatically.

They said therefore to Him, "What shall we do, that we may work the works of God?" Jesus answered and said to them, "This is the work of God that you believe in Him whom He has sent."

—John 6:28-29 (New American Standard)

YOUR TURN

What's your immediate response when you make a mistake? Acknowledgement? Apology? Denial?

When someone loves you, what responsibilities do you have toward him or her?

What responsibilities do you have to Jesus?

CHAPTER TWENTY-FIVE

LETTING GO

When I was 26 and a young head basketball coach at Iowa, I had a lot of confidence in myself as a coach. Maybe too much – but I was trying to fill Bucky O'Connor's shoes. At the end of the first semester of the 1960-1961 season, our team had recently ranked fifth in the country. We had the makings of a good, good team. I was on top of the world. But then I found out, at the semester break, that four of my starting players were ineligible due to academic performance. One was in pharmacy school and had just failed a course. Another guy, a smart guy, just froze up on tests.

My stomach dropped when I heard the news, as if I were strapped into one of those old roller coasters. I tried to put on bravado for my team, saying, "We've just got to suck it up and play our best, guys." But inside, I was frustrated, disappointed and scared. Our first game of the semester, against Indiana, was one week away and I was basically playing with a new team. We weren't that deep a team to begin with, and now we were in serious trouble.

I'd like to think I was worried for my players, but I was young and worried mostly for myself. How humiliating would it be to get blown out? How would I recover from this? I was looking at the possibility of losing to Indiana by 30 points – my estimate.

I finally had to admit that I just couldn't handle this situation myself. I started to look outside myself that week as I prepared the team for Indiana. I told God I wasn't able to do this on my own. I said, "I need help." I wasn't asking Him for a win. I needed strength and – if He saw fit – to be spared a career-changing blowout.

That week, I realized that my four replacements listened better than just about any players I had coached. My other players stepped up, too, as we centered our offensive strategy on Don Nelson (most recently he was with the NBA Golden State Warriors, and is the winningest coach in NBA history) and braced ourselves for whatever waited for us in Indiana. I just kept asking for help and admitting that I didn't have all of the answers. It was hard to admit, and harder to let go. I was thinking I ought to plan on staying in Indiana after the game, just so I wouldn't have to show my face in Iowa again.

Well, we showed up. We played. My players exceeded their capabilities and followed coaching instructions as I tried to stay calm.

With four minutes left in the game, I distinctly remember turning to Dick Schultz (my assistant coach, who later became executive director of the NCAA and subsequently the head of the U.S. Olympic Committee) and saying, "Don't tell me we have a chance to win this." We were up by seven. I can't describe my amazement and gratitude. When we won the game, I was completely stunned.

The rest of the semester went well for Iowa. The team kept exceeding their limitations, and played beyond their abilities. I learned that letting go and admitting, "I need help – I need God to help me handle this," is a powerful strategy for life. If we had lost that day in Indiana, my developing faith in God would have helped me through it. And when we won, by some kind of miracle, I realized that the *real* miracle here was how a young coach's spiritual journey can unfold while he's busy watching the score.

And my God shall supply all your needs according
to His riches in glory in Christ Jesus.

—Philippians 4:19 (New American Standard)

YOUR TURN

When is the last time you asked for help or guidance from Jesus?

What lessons have you learned from the unexpected miracles in your life?

CHAPTER TWENTY-SIX

GAME CHANGERS

Since I was part of basketball's "Fab Five" at the University of Iowa, I thought I might try professional basketball after graduation. There was something called the National Industrial Basketball League back then, a semi-pro league with teams sponsored by major U.S. companies. They would bring college grads into their company training programs to work for the company and play basketball for its sponsored team. Sounded pretty good to me. I liked the people in Akron – the Goodyear Tire & Rubber team.

I also felt a bit of pressure to go to law school. My brother did. A lot of my friends did. I can say now that I'm really, really glad I didn't.

Then, as a junior at the University of Iowa, I was asked to consider staying on as an assistant coach for both basketball and baseball. I couldn't turn down the chance to be an assistant coach at 22 years old. Besides, it was Bucky asking. The plan was that Bucky O'Connor would coach for 10 more years and then become athletic director and I would take over as head coach. Back then, being an athletic director was different from what it is now: less politics and financial chaos, more sports development.

If things had gone according to Bucky's plan, I would have inherited the head basketball coaching job at 32. I could see the next 20 years of my life ahead of me, planned perfectly, and it looked pretty good.

Then things went tragically wrong. Bucky was killed in a car accident. I was plunged into the head coaching position at 24 – the youngest coach in NCAA Division I history. I could handle the X's and O's of basketball and had a good rapport with our players, but I had a lot to learn about the politics of big-time athletics.

The next six years were thrilling, scary and exciting. I loved coaching the Hawkeyes. And coaching sports, like playing sports, can become an important part of your identity. So when I moved on from the University of Iowa, I found ways to stay involved in basketball while working on my real estate development business.

I became active with the Fellowship of Christian Athletes (FCA), worked as a color commentator for Iowa Basketball on WHO Radio (1966-1980), worked as a color commentator for KWWL, Iowa Television Network (1980-1985), and eventually served as a part-time coach for the Athletes in Action (AIA) basketball team. I loved that I was able to keep coaching and keep myself in basketball while running my business.

So when the head of AIA, Wendel Deyo, asked me to join the group full-time as head basketball coach, my first reaction was a big "No." I was a businessman. I had a drive to be wildly successful in real estate development. I was working in commercial real estate and my ego needed to keep working toward my big comeback! But after about four or five months of prayer, I realized that this opportunity was in line with many of my core values. And, while I always loved keeping lots of balls in the air, Kathy convinced me that I couldn't expect to do a great job simultaneously on both real estate and full-time coaching.

I accepted the position and learned what it meant to raise my own salary in a nonprofit organization. But I was coaching full-time again and I loved it. We played preseason exhibition games against top Division I teams such as Bobby Knight's in Indiana, Kentucky,

Michigan State, Purdue, Louisville, and Georgia Tech, to name a few. I loved seeing whether we could beat those great teams.

I didn't realize then what a tight grasp I had on coaching (and vice versa) until a fateful Friday night, a half-decade later. Wendel took me to dinner and stunned me by asking, "How would you like to leave coaching and become the general manager of Athletes in Action Basketball?" I replied, "Well, I really like coaching." That was an understatement! Again, my first reaction was to say, "No." Wendel said, "Would you go pray about it tonight?"

So I prayed. I said, "OK, Lord, if you want me to do this, you've got to release the grasp I have on coaching. My grasp is a lot bigger than I thought it was." I envisioned myself holding a basketball, having a tight control over it.

The next day, I prayed again: "God, you have to take this out of me or I don't think I can do what I've been asked to do."

And the next morning, Sunday, I woke up and didn't feel the grasp anymore. My hand felt wide open, like the basketball was just sitting in my hand. No more tightness.

I called Wendel and told him, "If this is what you want me to do, I'll give up coaching and be the GM." As much as I loved coaching, I've never felt remorse for this decision. God took the tight grasp away from me and I've never second-guessed it.

Leaving dreams behind to pursue new dreams is just part of life. Basketball, baseball, coaching, real estate, coaching (again), and even working at AIA were all important steps in my journey to start Basketball Club International (BCI), which is an extension of the change I want to see in the world. It is an extension of the work I've done and have yet to do in Christ's name.

Don't be afraid of change, and be mindful about what you're grasping and why, and what's got a grip on you. It can be helpful to ask God to help you release the grip and see the bigger picture. And it never hurts to say, "Let me pray on that and get back to you," before giving an answer to life's big opportunities.

The effective prayer of a righteous man can accomplish much.

—James 5:16 (New American Standard)

YOUR TURN

What "game-changing" moves have you made in your life?

Have you ever used prayer to help you make the transition?

CHAPTER TWENTY-SEVEN

IMPACT

God was up in heaven, making Adam. The angels watching Him said, "Lord, you've screwed up. You made a man but left a big hole in his heart. A big void." God turned to the angels and said, "You're right, I left a hole. It's just big enough for me. A God-shaped vacuum. Now the only way he'll be complete is if he puts me in his heart."

I think we all have the potential to experience, personally, the powerful impact of Jesus. We're born with a place in our hearts just for Him. At some point we're old enough to start learning and asking questions. Sometimes our parents help us with that, but more often it's our peers and our nonfamily mentors who step up to guide us toward our own personal relationship with the Lord.

In my family, my mom kept us going to church and youth group. It seemed like a good and wholesome part of our lives, but it wasn't so much spiritual as it was habit. Dad was a Catholic, but he didn't talk much about it. This was before so many churches taught about the personal relationship we can have with Jesus. It wasn't until I was in my late 30s that I started really seeking a deeper relationship with Jesus. But even before that, while coaching at the University of Iowa, I began to make myself available to the next generation of seekers.

One of the early Fellowship of Christian Athlete (FCA) conferences was held in Lake Geneva, Wisc., just north of the Illinois border. I was a young coach then, about 26. They asked all of the young coaches to lead small "huddle sessions," where the 400 kids at the conference would split up into smaller groups. I led evening sessions with my assigned huddle group, but I wasn't getting across to the kids at all. I couldn't understand why, and I didn't like that feeling.

Bob Watson, my friend and an assistant football coach at the University of Iowa, could tell I was discouraged. He said, "Sharm, you're taking too much on yourself. You're just here to be the conduit. Let the Lord use you in talking with these kids. Let your faith be the center, let Jesus be the center. Don't *you* try to be the center of attention!"

I told him I'd sleep on it. I hadn't realized I was making it a "me" kind of thing by worrying about how I was being perceived. What a wake-up call!

Brian Sternberg set a great example when he gave his testimony at the FCA Conference the same year. He once held the U.S. pole-vaulting record, but in a freak trampoline accident, he came down on his neck and was paralyzed from the neck down. He was down to about 100 pounds when he addressed us. After a tremendously inspiring testimony from his wheelchair, he said, "I would never wish this upon any of you out there." Then, after a long pause, he continued, "Unless it would take an accident like this to bring you to a faith in Christ." The room, filled with hundreds of adolescents and young adults, was completely silent. Brian had taken his situation and turned it around so that the focus – and our focus – was on faith.

A few years after I became active with the FCA, my brother Tom introduced me to Young Life. He said, "You ought to take a look at this. It's not unlike FCA in some ways, but it includes girls. You ought to take a group of kids out to a camp." Then – and this was definitely the Lord at work – three other guys mentioned Young Life to me that same spring. One was Jim Chapman, who ended up becoming president of a small Eastern college. Another was Jerry Williams, who played ball with me and was on the staff at the University of Iowa.

I thought, if four people, who know me well, including Tom, think this is a good idea; there must be something to it. We formed a little committee and started our own Iowa City Young Life chapter. We started by taking 13 kids to a camp in Buena Vista, Colo. Being in the real estate industry, I was the only one of the group with the flexibility to go on many of these trips. I ended up being both a chaperone and mentor. Bill Russell (not the Celtics player), Mike Petrak, and Andy Code were among the many involved at the same time I was. My brother, Tom, served on Young Life's national board.

I feel that through FCA, Young Life, AIA and now BCI, I've found unique opportunities to help young people realize the impact of Jesus in their lives. It's been a real privilege to serve in this way, sharing what I've learned and figured out over 76 years. But even as a young coach at 26, I had something to offer, even if it took a football coach to revise my playbook mid-game.

Neither he who plants nor he who waters is anything, but only God, who makes things grow. The man who plants and the man who waters have one purpose, and each will be rewarded according to his own labor.

—1 Corinthians 3:7-8 (New International Version)

YOUR TURN

Which of your experiences could you use to help make an impact in someone's life?

What impact has Jesus made in your life, and in the lives of people you admire or love?

CHAPTER TWENTY-EIGHT

SOON, BUT NOT YET

I was raised in a Lutheran home in the shadows of Augustana College, a Lutheran college. We went to church every Sunday, and I was confirmed in that church. I kind of enjoyed church, but not in a meaningful way. As a teenager, I participated in youth group some evenings. I was a good kid, but I would sometimes pocket the collection plate money my parents gave me and spend it on bubble gum down at the corner store with some of my buddies.

When I went off to Iowa, I'd try to go to church sometimes, especially when I wasn't busy traveling with the team. I'd try to get friends to go with me. Attending church wasn't a top priority, but it made the list.

My coach, Bucky O'Connor, went to the same church I did. But when he was killed, I felt as if I were suddenly on my own. I was 24 and started going to our church more regularly. I knew there had to be something more to this faith thing, but I was in a spiritual limbo. I was caught between the routine faith of a child and the deep faith of a man.

My first wife and I went to church every Sunday – the way my mom had us go. I even filled a spot on the church's board for three years. Then I was elected for four more years at Gloria Dei Lutheran Church in Iowa City. But always in the back of my mind was the thought, "There's got to be more than what I'm getting out of it." Then, spending some time with the Fellowship of Christian Athletes brought it a little closer to the front.

Over the years, I continued to deepen in my faith and commitment to God, but I was missing something: a personal relationship with Jesus. I knew, deep down, it was there waiting for me. I just wasn't ready to figure out how to reach it.

My teammate Carl Cain and I stayed in touch through the years after college. After collecting that Olympic gold medal we'd all dreamed about, but at the same time enduring a back injury that forced him to retire from basketball, Carl settled in the Midwest with his wife and daughters.

During one call, around 1979, Carl sounded different. I told him, "You're not the same. What's wrong?" He wouldn't say. But the next time we talked, he told me he'd hit a personal rock bottom. He'd made mistakes, he was depressed, he thought his life was headed nowhere, and he hadn't known what to do about any of it. Thankfully, his sister led him to the Lord. She told him, "You've got to accept Christ." And when he did, he was finally able to climb out of that hole.

Now, once you've escaped an abyss like that, you want to share the details with everybody in your life. Carl started telling me, "Sharm, I know you've given some of your life to God through Jesus, but Jesus wants all of your life, not just part of it." I'd say, "I know, I know. But not right now."

Every time we talked, he'd ask, "How's it coming?" I'd say, "It's coming, but not quite yet. Soon, Carl. But not yet." This line of conversation continued, about once a month, for around a year and a half.

After my divorce, I enjoyed the single lifestyle. I enjoyed spending time with my kids. I liked having time to work. I was never the most talented guy in the room, but I was often the hardest worker. I liked the idea of being a self-made man. I wasn't focused on my relationship with Jesus. I was pretty much distracted.

Then I met Kathy and, suddenly, I felt as if the game clock was running. I absolutely knew that I couldn't get married again until I'd given my life to Christ. I felt I needed to finish what I'd started on this journey of faith. So, just as I'd promised my mom I wouldn't get married until I graduated from college, I promised God I wouldn't remarry until I committed myself 100% to His Son.

"Okay Carl," I said. "Really soon now."

It still took a while to give my life fully to Jesus. I wanted to make sure the decision was the right one – the God-centered, Christ-centered choice.

I remember driving to Cedar Rapids, Iowa, listening to the radio, when I had to pull over. I was overwhelmed by something I'd heard. I was crying. And I knew it was time to let this happen. I was born again in Christ and, then, I asked Kathy to marry me. I told her, "I'm going to give my life completely to the Lord." We were both ready to be in this life, this faith, together, and it's been a wonderful 29 years (and counting).

So don't be so surprised when I tell you that you have to be "born from above"– out of this world, so to speak. You know well enough how the wind blows this way and that. You hear it rustling through the trees, but you have no idea where it comes from or where it's headed next. That's the way it is with everyone "born from above" by the wind of God, the Spirit of God.

– John 3:7-8 (The Message)

YOUR TURN

What parts of your spiritual life have you been putting off? Why?

How has your relationship with God changed since you were a child?

CHAPTER TWENTY-NINE

LOOKING UP

I like to ask youths about their plans. A few years ago I met a kid named Jeremy at a summer youth leadership summit in Alabama. He told me he wanted to play Division I basketball in college. I immediately replied, "OK, how are your grades?" He said he was getting C's and D's. I told him, "You're not gonna make it." Very, very few players are outstanding enough to get recruited with near-failing grades. Jeremy would need to make some changes. He looked as if I'd just hit him on the side of the head.

We kept in touch by e-mail and he wrote me at the end of the fall semester to say he'd earned all A's and B's. Now, I met this boy's parents and they seemed like good people. I'll bet they had tried to get their son to focus on his grades for years. But hearing it from me – or from a pro-level player, or from anyone who's actually been in the world he fantasizes about – is what finally made an impression. Jeremy is a smart kid, but he didn't know how to begin making decisions toward the future he wanted.

A lot of people wait and wait for some kind of spiritual epiphany, the same way some hope the NBA will knock on their mother's door. They may wait their whole lives. I think every life has moments that are especially moving – I've certainly had a few of those – but a relationship with Jesus isn't something you click on (or off) like a porch light.

It's more a matter of building that relationship over time, like anything else, which is why "relationship" is such a great word for it.

As my relationship with Jesus deepened over time, I began to feel compelled to use what I've been given in a way that would please Him, celebrate Him, and help others to see what a relationship with Him will offer. I just meet people wherever they are, even if they've never even considered a spiritual concept. I just talk about integrity, faith, values and basketball. We can all find common ground and start from there – a first step on a long journey.

So many kids and young adults seem to be floundering in the woods, unsure which way is "True North." I started Basketball Club International and the BCI Edge team because I care about these guys. I want them to have strong, worthy heroes to inspire them. I want their heroes, the pro players, to feel supported as role models, player-to-player. I want more basketball professionals to step up and mentor both kids *and* their heroes. We play games overseas to promote goodwill, we host youth basketball clinics and camps, we participate in events to support great youth-outreach organizations, and we promote player-to-player fellowship at the professional level. To me, this is Generation Hero. Anyone can be a part of it, just by starting a conversation about what's possible in the world, and how it can be influenced through basketball. And by remembering to look up.

Christ's love compels us.

– 2 Corinthians 5:14

YOUR TURN

What do you feel compelled to do for others?

How do you want your life to count?

CHAPTER THIRTY

REFLECTIONS

One player is so free-spirited that he takes crazy shots, confusing his teammates. Sometimes throwing a shot out of his tail works out, which just eggs him on. The coach has to say, "Look, I don't want to take away your individual spirit here, so you can have two wild shots this half. If you take a third, you're out."

Another player is steady, consistent, and a good listener. When he's on the court, in the middle of a play, he's pretty good. But his focus is too often somewhere else. He's multitasking. The coach has to remind him, "I know this isn't your number one passion right now, but pay attention to what you're doing while you're doing it."

There are so many temperaments and personalities on any court, especially at the college level. There are many temperaments within a lifetime, too, as you lose the carefree attitude of youth and gain the wisdom of age.

I transitioned away from childhood pretty quickly when my father passed away. I went from digging a trench just to play "war" with my brother (using jigsaw-cut "guns") to hanging out with teenagers and quickly becoming one. I even tried to smoke once, but only once – a corn silk cigarette, made from the stringy stuff you pull from inside of a corn husk. It was cheaper than tobacco and pretty terrible. The six puffs I tried at Carl Wickstrom's cabin didn't work out so well for me. Some of my friends drank a little – not much – while we played pool.

In high school, I played softball and baseball. One of my teams was part of a bar league, with older guys. Brandy's Tavern was our sponsor and we'd all get beer tokens after every game (despite my youth). I gave mine to the older guys in exchange for Orange Crush tokens. I was very popular with the older guys, because they liked the exchange.

One summer I worked for a construction company in the railroad yards of East Moline, Ill. My job was unloading 98-pound bags of cement. At the end of the day, I'd come home and just lie in the grass in our yard for quite a while – fully exhausted.

In college, I worked summers for the Iowa-Illinois Gas & Electric Co. I had a full athletic scholarship to the University of Iowa, so this was my extra spending money. My crew, mostly older guys, installed gas service in new homes. I made $1.38 an hour one year and $1.44 my final year. My crew liked me because I had energy. They'd have to slow me down, saying, "Hey, we don't want to overdo our quota. Take it easy for a while!" I know my work ethic was strong because of my dad. He taught me that working hard was just the right thing to do and I took that to heart.

I don't know whether Dad was a Christian when he passed away. I hope so. I just know that I wish he'd been able to be there for my high school and college basketball careers. He would have loved coming with us on the road trips. Sometimes I just break down thinking how we both missed out on that. Instead, my mom came with us, as one of four or five parents who tried to travel with the Hawkeyes.

I had to say goodbye to my father before I was a man. But when it was time for my mother to be called home, I'd been a man – and a man of faith – for a long time. She got to see the way that my brother, Tom, and I had not only deepened in our faith, but also formed personal relationships with Jesus Christ. I think it helped her grow, and got her out of her "church thinking." It was easy to talk to her about anything. In 2 Corinthians 4-5, the Bible talks about how as you grow older, your body starts to decay, but your spiritual faith grows. I think that's what happened, and it always made me feel good to know Tom and I were able to inspire her.

I suppose that between basketball and business, young marriage and children, Kathy and BCI, I've achieved a good balance between the free-spirited aspects and the steady aspects of my personality. I've learned so much about myself since Jesus became part of my life. I respect the simplicity of life and see things how they are. Getting older isn't boring. Quite the opposite.

When Coach Bucky was killed, I lost another piece of my youth, another mentor. But, over the years, I've been blessed with the opportunity to become a mentor to others. I'm still busy. I have more things going on now, with BCI, than I ever would have thought possible at 76 years old. And looking back on my life, I wouldn't have changed much at all. Every step was important – part of God's plan to bring me here. And here, today, is all I have. In this moment, I feel blessed by His grace.

"For I know the plans that I have for you," declares the Lord, "plans for welfare and not for calamity to give you a future and a hope. Then you will call upon Me and come and pray to Me, and I will listen to you. And you will seek Me and find Me, when you search for Me with all your heart."

—Jeremiah 29:11-13 (New American Standard)

YOUR TURN

When you reflect on your life, whether you are young or older:

What is the foundation of your life?

Do you have a spiritual foundation?

I Stand By the Door… An Apologia For My Life

By Sam Shoemaker

I stand by the door.
I neither go too far in, nor stay too far out.
The door is the most important door in the world-
It is the door through which men walk when they search and find God.
There's no use my going way inside, and staying there,
When so many are still outside and they, as much as I,
Crave to know where the door is.
And all that so many ever find
Is only the wall where a door ought to be.
They creep along the wall like blind men,
With outstretched, groping hands.
Searching for a door, knowing there must be a door,
Yet they never find it…
So I stand by the door.

The most tremendous thing in the world
Is for men to find that door-the door to God.
The most important thing any man can do
Is to take hold with tone of his blind, groping hands,
And put it on the latch - the latch that only clicks
And opens to the man's own touch.
Men die outside that door, as starving beggars die…
On cold nights in cruel cities in the dead of winter-
Die for want of what is within their grasp
They live, on the other side of the door-
Live because they have not found it.

Nothing else matters compared to helping them find the door,
As for me, I take my old accustomed place,
Close enough to God to hear Him and know He is there,
But not so far from men as not to hear them,
And remember they are there too.
So, I stand by the Door!